COACH YO
SUC

Tom Preston

2000

*This book is dedicated to Annie and Peter Preston –
with love and thanks.*

First published in 2009 by Management Books 2000 Ltd
Forge House, Limes Road
Kemble, Cirencester
Gloucestershire, GL7 6AD, UK
Tel: 0044 (0) 1285 771441
Fax: 0044 (0) 1285 771055
Email: info@mb2000.com
Web: www.mb2000.com

British Library Cataloguing in Publication Data is available

ISBN 9781852526146

Quotes and Testimonials

My career in football has left me in no doubt of the value of coaching. Executive coaching provides the same value to the business community. Tom's book will help you get to the top of your league.

David Dein
former Vice-Chairman, Arsenal Football Club

This book is powerful, engaging, full of colour and compelling.

Richard Greenhalgh
former Chairman, Unilever Plc

No matter how high-octane your performance is already, this book will raise your game another notch. A potent tool, full of great ideas for anyone with professional responsibility.

Elizabeth Littlefield
Director, The World Bank, Washington DC

An impactful, yet easy to digest, guide to the world of coaching.

Emma Bennett
Business School, Leadership Institute, Credit Suisse, London

Given the economic doldrums we are now facing, this is the time for many a manager to reflect on how they can become transformational leaders. *Coach Yourself to Success* is exactly that – a self help mirror you can read at your own pace and in your own time, with Thomas at your side, every step of the way. A must read for any leader wanting to stay at the top of their game.

Gustavo Antonioni
Commercial Brands Director, ITV Global Entertainment Ltd

Today's business reality demands a new vision of successful leadership of people. Never before has the understanding and ability of how to coach people to want to perform at their best been as crucial. This book is invaluable in unlocking the secrets to these skills.

Alistair Bradley
Managing Director, Danone Baby Nutrition – Austria

The idea of world beating athletes competing in the Olympics without a coach is laughable. In this book, Tom Preston demonstrates why the same thinking should be applied to top business management and brings the subject to life with his own very personal anecdotes.

Richard Hill
Executive Vice-President and Chief Financial Officer, Standard
Chartered First Bank – Korea

A stand-out book with direct application value. Executive coaching has never made as much sense, nor been as relevant to employers and employees alike – especially in the financial industry.

Philip Eisenbeiss
Partner, Executive Access Ltd, Hong Kong

For the simple cost of this book the owner will have access to practical activities, self-reflection tools and coaching techniques that would, in any other format, cost many thousands of dollars.

Jackie Darr
Director of Human Capital, Stark Investments, USA

Having benefited from executive coaching building my first and second businesses, I can strongly recommend Coach Yourself to Success to anyone wanting smart tactics and thought challenges to achieve professional and life clarity.

Suzanne Aaronson
Co-Founder, Spire.com

Tom is a truly remarkable Executive Coach. This book is just as remarkable as it will help businesses understand coaching, develop managers as leaders and coaches and be an invaluable text book for those wishing to learn the art of coaching.

Kim Morgan
Managing Director. Barefoot Coaching

To be what we are and to become what we are
capable of becoming is the only end in life,
Robert Louis Stevenson

Acknowledgements

There are so many people who deserve acknowledgement for contributing to the journey that has led to this book. However, there are some people I would like to thank specifically:

Our team at Thomas Preston & Associates: Jenni Sivertsen, Derek Wilson, Peter Thompson, Adrienne Percival, Alison O'Mahony, Julie Stokes, Jodie Gibbens and David Scotland. You have all taught me so much and I know that we have one of the best teams in the world delivering to our clients.

All of our clients – truly great human beings and organisations understand that reaching our full potential comes from within but is often nurtured and stimulated by objective external professionals. Thank you for your trust.

Kim Morgan and John Webster for the best training an Executive Coach could get.

Peter Hardy, Gretchen Worth and Sheila McNamara for helping me get this book written and edited.

Jonathan Lloyd, Camilla Goslett and the folks at my agents, Curtis Brown, and Nick Dale-Harris and the team at Management Books 2000.

Contents

Contents

Contents

Preface

Thomas Preston is the founder of Thomas Preston & Associates – one of Europe's leading executive coaching firms. The company has a broad client base of some of the world's best known companies. Thomas himself has worked with some of today's most influential business leaders in Britain, Germany, Belgium, France, Spain, the United States, and across Asia.

Before training to be an executive coach, his career saw him working in Africa and the Middle East as a commodity trader, then as the managing director of a private equity business in Hong Kong and as the chief operating officer of a boutique investment bank in Hong Kong and Taiwan.

All of that experience convinced him that pressured executives really needed a professional, trained and qualified thinking partner to help them better navigate the treacherous waters of modern business – and if they can't get qualified external coaching, they need self-help.

Thomas wrote *Coach Yourself to Success* to give anyone with professional responsibility access to the advantages of coaching. The book is specifically designed to allow the reader to coach him or herself in much the same way as they would be coached professionally were they to employ a coach.

As you read, you are constantly asked to investigate and evaluate how you can apply the book to your own life and career. The reader is given direct access to many of the psychological tools that professional coaches use to help them coach themselves and others – hence *Coach Yourself to Success*. The book is invaluable for personal use and also as a guide for the coaching others.

Coach Yourself to Success is a life manual. Readers are invited to return to its pages again and again, reminding themselves of how they might use a different approach each time that they tackle a new issue in their careers or relationships.

The design is such that the reader can easily dip in and out of chapters or whole sections – and it is highly interactive. You are constantly asked to apply the themes and concepts of the book proactively to you own situation.

1

Where to Begin

'Experience is not what happens to a man; it is what a man does with what happens to him.'
Aldous Huxley

Hello. My name is Tom. While you read this book, I am going to be your executive coach. My intention is to change your life for the better, quite simply, immediately and forever.

My job is to start you on the road to greater success. I will encourage you to look at your life, both personally and professionally, in an entirely different way.

There are plenty of self-help books on the market. There are even a couple of really quite good technical books on coaching. Yet until *Coach Yourself to Success*, there was no guide to give you the context and skills for you to coach yourself and others to higher performance. There was no book that clearly explained what makes executive coaching such a valuable proposition to all organisations and people, like you, with professional responsibility.

So let's embark on this journey together. I'll walk beside you, I'll indicate the direction you should go, but I'll not lead the way. That's for you to do, once I have taught you how to do it. But firstly, let me show you why the journey is necessary.

Perhaps you are now wondering whether or not you even need to work on achieving your potential? Well, take a few moments to carefully consider the following questions and tick the appropriate boxes:

Question	Yes	Not sure	No
1) Can you accurately state what you want from your life?			
2) Do you have a clear game plan for achieving what you want from your life?			
3) Does this game plan accurately pinpoint when you will achieve what you want?			
4) Does your present approach to the hurdles of work and home always assist you and motivate you?			
5) Are you confident that the current way in which you manage your career will fulfil all your personal and professional goals?			
6) Do you always manage your emotions and reactions to events in an entirely positive way?			
7) Are you operating consistently at the peak of your potential?			
8) Are you taking appropriate responsibility for your relationships – both personal and professional?			
9) Coaching today is an essential management skill for anyone with professional responsibility. Do you have all the coaching tools you need for maximum performance in your job?			
10) Are you satisfied that your management of yourself and others is as good as it could possibly be?			

If you have answered 'Yes' to any of the above questions, please write your answer on a piece of paper. For example, to question 1 write: 'What I want from my life is.......'

When you have done that, ask yourself the question again and check that you would again tick the Yes box in the questionnaire.

If you have answered 'No' or 'Not Sure' to more than one of these ten questions, read this book carefully. It promises to revolutionise your life.

Now consider the following:

Business is not a lottery. Nor is your life.

You can choose to succeed, just as you can choose to be happy. In business as in life, you can choose to stand still or to move forward. You can also choose to fail.

Of course, external factors can play a significant part. But, on the governing level, the choice is entirely yours.

Suppose, for a moment I were to tell you that for a nominal financial investment and a few hours of your hard-pressed time you could increase your company's profitability almost overnight by, say, 40%. What would that actually mean in financial terms both to your business and to your own personal bank account?

It's your company, department or responsibility, not mine. You do the maths.

No way, José

Would you listen? Of course, you would. A magician with a pack of cards and a genie with a lamp will always command an audience.

But even before I begin to explain, you have inwardly dismissed the idea. You discard the idea instinctively as the stuff of pipe dreams. We're all hard-wired to conventional reason.

A little voice inside you cautions: 'It's just not possible. We know our business. We're already successful in our field, and we have a streamlined operation that works. So OK, a shrewd nip and tuck here and there might give us an extra 5%. But 40? No way.'

'To contemplate such a jump,' says the voice, 'we would have to recruit a completely fresh tier of senior management. Even if we could find such a rich vein of expertise, the cost in salaries alone would be unacceptably high, with no certainty of success. We don't have the resources. We wouldn't know where to look.'

Look in the mirror

Wrong. You don't need to look anywhere else. You already have the resources and they're staring you in the face. You – your executives, from company chairman to senior sales manager – you are the resources. All you have to do is to fully realise them.

Most executives are living and working at a maximum 40% of their ability. They're under-achieving on a massive scale. What I offer is a simple, effective and accountable way of tapping into this pool of performance. Imagine the financial effect if you could harness even half that potential for a fraction of what you spend on business class air travel or corporate entertainment.

The answer lies in executive coaching, a subject which has nothing to do with bussing the board and senior staff by road in leather-seated comfort from one place to another – although it is entirely about a change of view.

Go for gold

Think sports coaching. A Top 20 tennis player has a coach. He or she is not going to reach the second week of Wimbledon without one. A pro-tour golfer has a coach. An Olympic runner or swimmer has a coach. Tiger Woods has four coaches. Not a single one of these athletes expects to succeed without support.

Don't confuse support with assistance. It's the players, not their coaches, who are the runaway leaders in their fields. The coach's job is to point the way to the bolted door that leads to the path of improvement in swing, stride, or stroke. It's his job to point out the hidden choice of routes for getting the best out of your team or for tackling the opposition.

So why don't the top athletes of international business, the pro players on the corporate circuit, have coaches? The answer is that the persistent winners, the Roger Federers and the Tiger Woods of the financial forum, already do. Shouldn't you?

Whether a physical or a cerebral player, the higher the athlete climbs the ladder of success, the more isolated he or she inevitably becomes. On the upper rungs, that isolation becomes absolute. Quite simply, there's no-one to talk to who doesn't have their own agenda.

Peak performance

One of the penalties of peak performance or high office is the need to appear invincible, to be capable of handling any emergency, and always to be in control. The world does not expect a board member of a large quoted company to experience self-doubt or uncertainty. Yet these are human frailties common to us all, without exception.

Today, many of the world's top performers run businesses. They are members of corporate boards, management teams, partners in commerce and industry, in professional practices and entrepreneurs. Technology, globalisation, corporate transparency, multi-cultural, multi-national and multi-faceted jobs are the norm. Performance is all.

Executives are expected to master increasingly complex jobs with constantly rising performance expectations. But as these professionals take on more responsibility, the more difficult their task becomes. It can feel very lonely at the top.

Who do these people confide in? Who encourages them to think differently? Who protects their interests and careers? Who offers them that vital perspective on their world? Who nurtures their development and continued success?

Nowhere to turn

Often these high-flyers know they could do better, but they don't know how to improve or progress. Often they feel they cannot discuss their anxieties with their domestic partners for fear of burdening them with these unspoken fears.

They worry about the conflict between spending more time at work, more time with their family, more time getting fit, more time, more time, more time...

They can't talk to their superiors for fear of appearing less than capable.

They cannot confide in subordinates because it makes them seem vulnerable – these are the people who look up to them for leadership.

They can't trust colleagues in their peer group because they're competing with them for the next promotion.

Usually their friends are simply too busy with their own lives to have the time, interest or inclination to spend hours listening to what might appear to be an intractable set of problems with no relevance to the listener's own life.

Catch a coach

Work can be a daunting place without honest, objective and practical support from someone whose only concern is to protect, nurture and develop that executive – the executive coach. If you can't get external help, you must learn to coach yourself and those around you.

This tested method of support is widely used by some of the biggest companies and organisations in the world. These include Unilever, Citigroup, KPMG, Tesco, ABN Amro, and The World Bank. Global giants such as UBS now see executive coaching as an integral part of their management practice.

According to the American Psychological Association, the executive coaching market is worth £500 million a year. It's growing at an estimated 40% per annum and *The Economist* rates it as the fastest growing industry in Europe after IT.

Of course, it's not new. The Ancient Greeks were adept at it. If two athletes have identical latent talent what differentiates one from the other? One wins the race and one does not. This is where coaching comes into its own. For millennia, it has played a significant part in the creation of success.

Coaching is entirely flexible in its use and can be adapted to specific needs – whether you are seeking a new role, or better personal relationships with colleagues, customers, managers and stakeholders.

Resistance to the concept of coaching is slowly waning, particularly in the upper echelons of international business, where its benefits have been best felt.

Increasingly, to have a coach is regarded as a badge of honour.

What it means is that the company sees this employee as someone with the potential to go far in the organisation. Therefore they are willing to invest in order to maximise his or her potential – to allow them to reach greater success faster, to achieve higher job satisfaction, and a better life/work balance.

In an increasingly volatile job market, it is a clear sign that an employer is investing in this particular executive's ability and untapped potential. The motive is to want to retain and improve his or her performance and success. The better the coaching, the greater the ability of the performers to release their latent talent.

People power

Today we can each expect to have up to five different careers during our working life. Is it rational to think that man and woman can deal with such demands and expectations alone?

As management becomes less hierarchical an executive needs to improve 'soft' skills: the ability to motivate, lead, build teams and create effective relationships that make work enjoyable. It is all about people. Emotional quotient (EQ) has become as equally important as intellectual quotient (IQ).

We have established universities and libraries and umpteen other tools to develop intellectual quotient, but somehow the world has decided – until now – that development of an individual's emotional quotient should be left entirely to chance.

Corporations claim to care. They claim to have values of social responsibility. They claim to act in the interests of their stakeholders, their shareholders, their clients, their employees, and the communities in which they operate.

But the incontrovertible truth is that, above all else, corporations exist to make profits. This can conflict with a softer 'touch and feel' aspiration.

Who benefits?

So who should consider executive coaching? The short answer is anyone who has professional responsibility. It is equally beneficial to managers, doctors, lawyers, advertising executives, bankers, entrepreneurs, managing directors, media professionals, even rock stars.

From the recipient's point of view the case for coaching is clear. But what is the value-for-money equation for the corporation, the paymaster? It lies in improved performance, in job satisfaction, in retaining the best people, in enhancing skills that improve relationships, technical abilities and best practices. It lies in creating, nurturing and developing the very best professionals – the people who drive a company or organisation to success. Executive coaching helps them to adapt, to effectively manage change and to ultimately enhance their prospects of survival and prosperity by making profits and building shareholder value.

Remember that success in business and personal happiness are always choices. But each choice is also governed by the changing parameters of how we choose to interpret that success or happiness. What I term success today, I might not term as success in five years time. When I achieve one goal and reach out for the next, my definition of success is inevitably altered. What matters most is my positive state of mind.

Over the following pages I'm going to show you the way to that locked door to improvement. I'll put the key in the lock, but only you can turn it.

But let me make one important point absolutely clear. This book is not going to tell you anything that you don't already know. Your problem is that you don't know that you know it. What I can provide is that missing bridge to your subconscious, the catalyst to clarity of thought that can quite simply transform your work and, indeed, your whole life.

Coaching yourself

During the course of this book, I will ask you to audit your beliefs about yourself and investigate the forces that drive you. I want you to think carefully about whether in fact you should have far more confidence in yourself than you currently have.

You will learn ways in which you can identify what it is that you really want from your life and your career and how to achieve these goals. You will learn how to think differently about events and changes in your work or life. You will arm yourself with better relationship management tools and attain a clearer overall perspective.

So, even if you can't get a good coach to work with you, at least you will know how to apply sound coaching technique to yourself and those around you. To achieve this, think carefully as you read, how each chapter, each case study and each exercise applies to you and your life. Reflect.

A gift

This book is designed as a gift to you. It will allow you to understand the power of coaching. It will give you the insight needed to know how to use it and how flexible a tool it is.

It will allow you to choose to succeed and be more effective. It will make the doing so more fun and rewarding. You will learn tried and tested techniques to improve the quality of your life – to get more of what you want, both personally and professionally.

If you accept that real happiness comes from making life a competition in generosity of spirit, the greatest gift of all will be to enable you to share this gift with others.

Before you read on.....

Can I ask you to take a moment to imagine how wonderful you will feel when you know, clearly, what you want from your life – in the sure knowledge that you can choose your mood and your reactions to events and the people you encounter in life.

Imagine how good you will feel when you know that you have a map of your life that will help you to arrive at success – however you choose to define it. Reflect and enjoy the power of your imagination.

2

A Bit About Me

'Help! I need somebody. Help!
Won't you please, please help me?'
The Beatles

As your executive coach, I now need to break the cardinal rule of coaching – and talk about myself. This is the only occasion in this book when we will not be focused on the subject matter in hand. The coach's role is one of catalyst, and for clarity of focus it is normally best carried out under a cloak of personal anonymity. As the client, you really don't need to cloud your mind with any detail of your coach's private life because it's your life not his or hers upon which we are concentrating.

However, I am throwing away the rule-book on this occasion because I want you to understand how I could possibly have the audacity to think that I might be able to help you to become even more successful than you already are.

I believe that the practice of executive coaching is the single most powerful development tool available to professionals and to their organisations. To appreciate this you need to understand how I came to this conclusion and switched from a lucrative and successful international business career to become a full-time coach. It was a strange journey.

My career has taken me all over the globe and has to date been, I think it fair to say, eclectic. Others might be more forthright and simply call it weird.

I started my first serious job at 22. I was hired by a London-based sugar trader whose main market was in West Africa, notably Nigeria. At the time, the country had just experienced a *coup d'état* and trading was extraordinarily difficult against a backdrop of dangerously volatile security conditions.

Immediately prior to the coup, my new employer had shipped 28,000 tons of sugar to a trader whose operations were primarily based in Lagos. The coup had wrought havoc on his trading empire and his ability to pay for the millions of dollars worth of goods that were in transit when political turmoil struck.

The two consignments of sugar remained unpaid for. They were languishing along with an astonishing number of other perishable cargos aboard an international fleet of vessels stacked along the West African coast off Lomé in Togo.

Use your sugarloaf

My brief was simple: Forget Nigeria. Find a way for the two ships to dock at Lomé, locate a buyer, offload and sell the sugar, collect the cash – oh, and find a way of safely transferring the proceeds to our headquarters in London.

Looking back on the mission with the benefit of hindsight, I feel certain that my employer despatched me more in desperation than in serious expectation of success, a wild kick at the goal in the dying seconds of the game. But at 22, nothing is necessarily too daunting. I had a job to do, so I did it.

As I sat on the plane going to a place I had never heard of to do something of which I had absolutely zero experience, the enormity of the task ahead failed to strike me. I was – through the absence of any negative thoughts of failure – simply refusing to cower in the face of this new (to me) world of business in which so many people seemed to flourish and prosper.

Somehow I transferred the sugar, bag by bag, from ship to shore and to the women in the local market in Lomé. By the time I returned to London I had converted what I could of the two cargoes into $10 million, which I remitted to London by a circuitous route of Lebanese gold traders and Swiss banks.

For me it was a baptism of fire. Along the way, I found myself under house arrest by the Togo Minister of Commerce on spurious charges of import tax evasion and for the sake of personal survival I was pitched headfirst into an immersion course in the art of negotiation. I might have known then, had I felt the need to reflect upon the subject, that I was on the launching pad of an extraordinary and interesting career.

Sweet success

My ability to survive, even to flourish, professionally under such pressure seemed to impress my bosses. Over the next ten years I became the company's 'man in Africa' with overall responsibility for sales, shipping and administration for all commodity trading in 23 countries in Africa and the Middle East.

Within eight years I was part-owner of the business, a director in a company whose sales had surpassed US$100 million per annum. Yet my life was running increasingly out of control – and I had no idea what to do about it.

I was living alone in a large and comfortable flat in central London, but I was hardly ever there to enjoy it. Any form of satisfactory personal life was subjugated to work. I was jogging with no sense of destiny and an air of heightening futility on a treadmill of hotel rooms, airports, and boardrooms. I was spending nearly all my waking hours with a phone cradled to my head.

Once during a rare visit home to my flat, I was rudely awakened from a deep sleep at 4am by a call from Lagos. With as much enthusiasm as I could muster at that ungodly hour of the morning, I began to state my views on how we should offload a shipload of vegetable oil that was heading that way – not paid for, as usual.

The next thing I knew, I was vaguely aware of my client's voice over the receiver shouting 'Hello? Hello?' I had fallen asleep in mid-conversation and had been, apparently, snoring loudly.

Galloping towards oblivion

It was my defining moment of crisis, my road to Damascus – but one

27

without any spark of enlightenment. I knew when I finally put the phone down and before I sank back into broken slumber that I could not continue like this. I was a rider-less horse in the Grand National of commerce, jumping fence after fence without purpose or proper intent because I didn't know what else to do.

Above all, I didn't know where to turn for help. I had no concept of how to manage my career, let alone the way to protect and develop it. I had no idea of how to arrive at a reasonable balance between life and work, or how to get my job and my life into perspective in a way that made sense both for me, my colleagues and my bosses.

So I decided to quit.

To me, it was the only course of action that made any sense. To all the other options – and there are always more options than you initially imagine – I was blinkered. What I now know I needed desperately but didn't have – indeed, I had no idea that such a person existed – was an expert executive coach.

I told myself that firstly what I had to do was to realise as much cash as possible in order to embark on my new career – whatever that might be. I sold my lovely London flat at the bottom of a slump in the property market and set out to try and sell my shares in the company to which I had devoted so many years, shaping it into the success story that it had become.

The majority shareholders were members of an upright and moral family, which had played an important role in the international sugar trade for the past three centuries. Over the years that I had worked for them they had become – and thankfully remain – my close friends. If I was to sell my equity in the business they would have to agree to buy me out.

Although they raised no formal objection when I first mooted the idea of selling my equity to them, they were understandably reluctant. Rightly or wrongly, they saw me as the goose that had persistently laid the proverbial golden egg that had contributed largely towards the current success of the company.

They were caught on the horns of a dilemma. They were afraid that if they bought me out, I would leave. If, on the other hand, they declined to buy me out, they feared I would still leave. So they bought me out, and I left.

It need never have happened

If, years or even months earlier, they had thought to hire a coach for me – and for themselves – my decision to sell my shares might never have been reached. Even at that late stage they would in all probability have retained a key loyal employee and partner in the business. But none of us knew at the time of the existence of executive coaches.

They came up with an alternative solution. Why didn't I take a break from Africa and go to Kuala Lumpur where they had a vegetable oil trading office? I would learn commodity trading at a grass roots level and, at the same time, I could travel around the Far East scouring out new trading opportunities before returning, when I felt like it, to England.

I imagine they thought that, after my career break, I would return refreshed to London and would be ready once again to lay more of those golden eggs in Africa.

In fact, they were wrong. The more time I spent in Asia the more I was convinced that there was a wider world beyond Africa. After several months, as promised, I did return to the company headquarters in London, but only to put forward my proposal for the future.

My travels had taken me to Vietnam, which I considered to be the emerging tiger of the then roaring economies of the Far East. In Hanoi I had stumbled across a group of Australians who, with virtually no capital, had launched the first English language newspaper in the country since the Vietnam War.

A foreign Fleet Street

Unbeknown to my bosses in London, I had already agreed to buy a major shareholding in the publishing company. To me, it seemed an exciting and rewarding prospect to build a media empire in a one-party Communist state that had set its sights on becoming a developed nation by 2020. Certainly it was a far more challenging proposition than returning to the steaming commercial jungles of Africa. Unfortunately, my employers didn't see it that way.

Undaunted, I resolved to go it alone. I put up my entire life savings – the money from the sale of my London apartment and from my equity in the company. If my bosses could not see the wisdom in this scheme, then they – not me – were the losers.

However, all my money was nowhere near enough. The Australian mini media tycoons were astute and their price was high. I set about raising money from my work colleagues. One by one they bought into the idea: a few thousand pounds here, a few more there. It started to add up.

The river of cash slowly gathered momentum until it was unstoppable. Then came the day when the company chairman read an annual report from a prominent French bank containing pictures of a Vietnamese cyclo driver reading a copy of the newspaper. The company decided to invest.

Happy, broke and homeless

I had done it! But at a high personal cost. I had no home, and all the money I had accrued out of blatant capitalism was now invested in a communist country on the other side of the world. In my mind, I was already a media baron, but how much better this would have been – both from my own and from my company's perspective – if I had worked rather than stumbled through all these issues with the support of an executive coach?

Eventually, the company decided that our newspaper venture held sufficient promise to warrant the establishment of an office in Hong Kong to monitor our investment and seek out other opportunities.

So, to my delight, at the age of 31, I found myself on a plane going back to the Far East with a suitcase and a single aim: to establish a private equity business.

I learned on the job. Within 18 months we had sold our interests in the newspaper to Australian media tycoon Kerry Packer for a profit of over 100%.

In the hectic years that followed, we were on a permanent roll. We invested in the first international school in Ho Chi Minh City and sold for almost as a big a profit. We invested in a coffee roasting, grinding and packaging company in Guangdong Province in China. We invested in pan-Asian publishing businesses. We bought real estate in Shanghai, which we let at phenomenal rents. Success bred success – we doubled the fund available for investment by raising new capital from a major financial institution in Belgium.

If I am honest with myself, there was no grand design. All this just seemed to happen of its own accord. It was opportunistic and haphazard. Not for a single moment did I pause to take stock of what was happening around me. I did not realise that I was in the most fortunate and positive position in the world – nor that it was a positive position of my creation. Worst of all, it never occurred to me that I needed to manage this incredible position in order to ensure that it lasted for me and for my company.

Flying blind

All I knew was that some celestial after-burner seemed to have kicked in on my career and it was compelling me forward at a speed I could no longer control. I was still in the left-hand seat and in nominal charge of the aircraft, but most of the time I couldn't distinguish any horizon at all.

I wasn't thinking about how I was doing it, what I could do better, or what my huge responsibility really entailed. I was just doing it.

Fortunately, along the way, I had more than my fair share of luck. I met some extraordinary people who, watching me spin, decided to provide me with some help. They gave me the opportunity to talk issues over, offering gentle but sound advice. They were the people I turned to when I didn't understand or was afraid. They listened. Above all, they were available to listen. They encouraged me to find my own answers. And I am ever grateful to these people. But sadly, they were not trained executive coaches.

By now, I was sitting on the boards of some ten companies and I began to realise that some of my co-directors also needed support. They too were sometimes finding it hard to see the wood for the trees. They, too, were so involved in running their businesses that there were moments when they could not spot the most obvious and simple solutions to even basic business issues.

Occasionally they felt isolated, dissatisfied, unappreciated, or lost. Sometimes the voice in their heads was so loud it was deafening. Sometimes they smelt a rat but failed to act for fear that they were wrong. And all of them, from time to time, felt professionally lonely.

I started to realise that if I could fill some of these gaps I could make a real difference to the commercial performance of the companies with which I was involved.

I made a real effort to listen more, to be less critical and to encourage dialogue with my co-directors. I tried to spend more time questioning than telling. I wanted my colleagues to know that they could pick up the phone and talk to me in confidence, and that I would seek to be objective and to provide perspective.

This was all well and good, and certainly more effective than being the combative representative of a purely financial organisation. But, I was doing it intuitively, feeling my way in the dark. I still wasn't equating this to my own situation but, nevertheless, this was the early start of my career as an executive coach.

Nose dive

Then disaster struck. Having trouble with the controls and now unable to see the horizon, a crash was inevitable. One day I chose to totally ignore my intuition – the same intuition that had got me in the first place into this positive career position.

I met an entrepreneur who had the great idea to build China's first outdoor media business. He had the experience, the contacts and the contracts. On paper, this was the dream investment, the chance to hit a home run, to make hundreds of millions of dollars in a single well-planned coup. All we had to do was take a tried-and-tested business model and apply it to China, one of the fastest-growing consumer markets in the world.

The business was simple. We were going to install bus shelters, complete with light boxes, in all the major cities in China – and then sell the advertising space. Companies such as J C Decaux and Clear Channel Inc. had become billion-dollar companies from just such a simple idea.

The problem was that when I was introduced to the entrepreneur I had an intense and distinctly intuitive reaction. As I walked into the restaurant to meet him for the first time my mind, my whole body screamed: 'Do not trust this man!'

Yet I ignored my faithful intuition. In recompense, I sought and received the reassurance of others who supported the logic of the business and its potential. In other words, I allowed my own and other people's greed to take precedence over my gut reaction. What I did was to allow my conscious mind to discount and discredit my unconscious intuition.

Ten million US dollars later, after lodging a complaint with the Commercial Crime Bureau (Hong Kong's equivalent to the UK's City of London Police Fraud Squad), plus three years of sleepless nights and being exposed to considerable personal danger, my intuition had proved unequivocally correct. And my career was in tatters.

Rewriting history with the benefit of hindsight is an easy but fruitless task. If I had turned left instead of right at an early crossroads, if I had ignored a no-entry sign on that ruinous road map and pushed on regardless, things might or might not have turned out as they did. But I can with certainty say that if I had been working with a trained executive coach at the time, the way would have turned out very differently.

Jammed joystick

As the aircraft dipped towards ground, I lacked the basic tools to handle the escalating crisis. The worse matters got during the course of this investment, the narrower my perspective became. I had multiple choices – multiple potential courses of action – but the instrument screens were blank and hidden from view. As velocity increased I had less and less idea how to deal with it, and the same applied to the others trapped with me in the cockpit.

I was the captain, and the buck – or rather, in this case, 10 million bucks – stopped with me. I lost sight of what I wanted and what I needed to achieve – to find a way of levelling out the dive and restoring order. I was unable to protect the shareholders and stakeholders. I am the first to admit that I did not, in retrospect, handle the situation that arose in the best possible way.

'The definition of madness is to do the same thing over and over again and to expect a different result,' said Mae West, and she was right. I started to do the same things over and over again, each time expecting a different result. I bounced from one opinion to another, depending on the situation of the day, instead of having a clear set of objectives.

I lacked a box of reasoning tools and a clear timeframe in which to resolve the situation. I bear the burden of ultimate responsibility, but I was not alone. My fellow directors were equally dumbfounded by the drama in which we were all embroiled along with a couple of investment committees comprised of highly intelligent, seasoned financiers, and a host of professional advisors. The fact is that we all lost the plot – collectively.

Today I am convinced that had even one of us benefited from the support of an executive coach, we might have righted the dive and turned the flight into that elusive US$100 million profit.

It could have been that, with the insight opened to us by an executive coach, we would never have made that initial investment and saved the principal sum.

Who knows? What I do know is that I failed to see – and therefore to use – the wide choice of options that were available to me. I allowed misplaced emotion to cloud my judgment. I felt horribly stressed, miserably lonely, totally isolated and an unmitigated failure. And I now know that all this could have been avoided.

Moral support and meltdown

I was lucky, I had family and friends who listened, supported, and encouraged as I poured out my plight. The more I told them, the clearer my mind became. I saw what I needed to do to salvage as much as possible from the chaos.

While battling with our advertising disaster in 1997, Hong Kong was passing from British sovereignty to Chinese control. The ink was barely dry on the handover documents when the Asian financial crisis hit, bringing regional economic meltdown.

At the same time, the parent company that I worked for had a default in the vegetable oil market that cost millions of dollars, and suddenly the shareholders had had enough. I was asked to return to

London to restructure the group globally, and in completing this giant canvas I painted myself out of a job.

I returned to Hong Kong to set up a boutique investment banking company with two Chinese partners. Once again, I feel that if I had had support, plus someone encouraging me to establish clear goals and assess my responsibilities with perspective, this could have been a rewarding experience.

After 9/11 and the subsequent global slow-down, my two partners bought me out. The decision to go our separate ways was partly due to differences of opinion on the future direction of the business. It was also because, for the first time in my life and career, I was starting to ask the key question of myself: what did I really want?

Starboard home

I have to say that it came as a considerable surprise to learn that what I really wanted after ten years in Hong Kong was to return to Europe. The reasons were multi-faceted. I felt keenly aware of the passage of time. I had just experienced two consecutive intense, but equally disastrous, romantic relationships. I wanted the chance to build a life in Europe with a partner, and for us to enjoy a life together before it was too late.

I wanted to travel to parts of the world that I had not seen, either because I had never had the time or the financial resources. Having sold my shares in the business and determined to go back to Europe, I now had both.

I make this sound as if all these were conscious decisions. The truth is that they came about more as a result of osmosis and circumstance than as the result of careful planning and single-minded determination.

Had they come about through forethought, I am sure I would have planned better and used my time travelling more efficiently. No doubt I would have set about building a career in Europe with a far stronger sense of purpose.

I left Hong Kong for Bangkok where I lived for five months before drifting on at my leisure to Burma, Botswana, South Africa and a variety of interesting places in between.

Coach lights

Back in London I was vaguely thinking about what to do next. While I considered my options, I started consulting for one of Britain's leading Lifestyle PR companies and for a video company. My role involved motivating the managing directors of each concern to grow their businesses and to develop expansion strategies.

It was through this temporary placement that I finally met John Webster, the executive coach who was to change the course of my life. He was running a university training course for potential coaches. It took the strength and immediate benefits of a single meeting for me to understand the exciting principles of executive coaching. After all, it was what – without any training – I was already instinctively trying to practise.

I was immediately at ease with him. He asked me more questions than had ever before been fired at me in such a short time. I ran him through the highs and lows of my life. Soon he had a pen out and was writing down my career highlights. Things that I had thought very ordinary, he pinpointed and congratulated me on. The more questions he raised, the more clearly I could see the answers to what had only minutes previously been apparently insoluble problems. At the end of the session I knew irrevocably the answer to that original question: what did I really want?

I wanted to be an executive coach.

Some 18 months later I became one of the first academically trained executive coaches in Britain. This formal training, combined with my decades of top-level commercial experience, allows me to provide the kind of business support for others that I could only have dreamed of receiving in my own former career as a high-flying executive.

My life was again about to change and, as I had just discovered, life is all about change.

Before you read on.....

Pause here for a moment and consider how you would tell your own story to date.

What would have been the benefit to you of having had such a sounding board? How would it be different for you in the future if you had someone who was more objective about what has happened so far in your life and your career than you have been able to be?

Having thought about this, what would be the benefit to you of stepping out of your life for a moment and looking at it objectively – as if you were someone else?

What would have happened at important crossroads in your life if you had trusted your intuition or had a cerebral partner – in the vein that our relationship is heading – who could have helped you to think?

As your coach, I am asking you to do just that: to step out of your life for a little while and view it as if it were someone else's. It's not difficult to do. Address and study yourself in the third rather than the first person – it's not 'I', it's 'he' or 'she'. Jot down on a piece of paper the main points of your reflection and what 'he' or 'she' will do differently in future as a result of these thoughts.

And, by the way, thank you. You are taking this process seriously. I can't do the work for you – I can simply, as your coach, ask you the questions. The answers are always yours. The actions that follow are also entirely motivated by you.

3

Change

'The mind is slow to unlearn what it has been long in learning.'
Seneca

Change is the single most influential factor in business and is the anvil of executive coaching.

We are all hardwired to view change as a harbinger of chaos, and so it is. But not in the sense of the yawning chasm of confusion defined by the Ancient Greeks, but rather the new watchful dawning of the Chinese. In Mandarin, the word for chaos is formed of two characters: danger and opportunity.

Seek out the advantage it can offer. Change is no longer your enemy but your friend. Embrace it, don't resist it. Remember that the cause of change is insignificant in comparison to your attitude towards change.

My client George is the senior sales manager of a large and very successful computer software company. He has always excelled at his job. One day he arrived for a coaching session looking distinctly perplexed. He explained to me that he had cut costs as far as he could, yet the organisation had set even higher budgets for the year ahead. He was struggling to see how he could meet his profit target – there was simply nowhere left to cut costs or people.

I asked him to give me some ideas as to how he thought he might be able to make the numbers without further cuts. Gingerly he started to investigate territory that, to him, was uncomfortable. He said that the only way he could get to the new budget numbers would be to entirely change the way that his section of the organisation worked.

He would have to ask the heads of each business unit to find ways to increase revenues. But that would mean that they could no longer work independently of each other. They would have to think and act as a team. This would require George to radically alter his own management style. He would have to change from expert technician and analyst to inspirational leader. But the downside was that George thought that all that 'people' stuff was so much fluff, and he concluded that the change would never work.

Already answered

In fact, George had answered his own question. However, he had rejected the solution as it would require a change in him and, equally importantly, it would require his acceptance of that change.

As we talked more, and I asked more and more questions as to how he could achieve his budget, George became more and more convinced that if he could inspire his team through a different style of leadership then they – and he – could reach the required numbers.

By the end of the session, he had devised a plan of action. He had written an inspiring vision statement and thought that he could get his team to buy into it. George had not only committed to change but committed to personally taking control of the change that was needed to reach the company's goal.

Six months later George and his team were above budget, and he had transformed from being 'a pure numbers guy' to a manager who could truly lead his team.

What about you?

If you were George, or in a similar situation in your own business life, how quickly would you embrace such a change?

We all change all the time. When we are young we accept change as a normal part of life. As we get older, we find it more demanding to adapt to differing circumstances and even more difficult to create change within ourselves. With the passage of years, the need for change seems to diminish in our minds and we tend to accept that the status quo cannot be altered. That is a mistake – change is constant.

Consciously or unconsciously, most of us resist change. Familiarity is a comfortable cushion on which we are happy to lean back and relax. The unknown is necessarily daunting, but there is nothing we can do to keep things a certain way.

Speed of change

In today's fast-moving world, change is more apparent than ever. Communications and technology develop with breathtaking speed and spread further and faster than ever before. Globalisation now requires executives to stay abreast of developments as they happen anywhere in the world, and this results in the need for instant decisions that can have far-reaching consequences.

The events of September 11th, 2001 provided a tragic example of how our whole world can alter irrevocably in a matter of minutes.

What happened that day is fused into our memories. The attacks on the twin towers and on Washington DC exerted huge stress on almost every business around the globe. These events caused equities to plummet, bonds to rally, gold and oil to rise, and airlines to go bankrupt.

Within minutes, this act of social and economic war virtually paralysed America, divided Europe, signalled the military invasion of two countries, and altered the course of millions of lives. How could anyone have understood or predicted the extent of change that would occur in the months and years that have followed?

Yet somehow we have to get used to the fact that change on a major scale is increasing at a gathering pace. Companies and business leaders need to be increasingly adaptable. Decisions often have to be made at the speed of light to stay ahead of the game, protect companies, and safeguard shareholders and staff.

Frequently an organisation's very survival depends on its ability to move with the times. Because change is such a permanent fixture in life, leaders have a critical need to embrace it and turn it to their advantage through skilled and visionary management.

Change in China

One of the most remarkable changes in recent history – and there have been many – took place in 20th-century China. A highly bureaucratic, regimented country with a state-controlled economy mutated into an economic powerhouse on a global scale in less than three decades.

It was transformation on an unimaginable scale that occurred in a short period of time. It involved many millions of people, yet it was achieved with a minimum of fuss or upheaval, and it has had startling results.

Thirty years ago, it was a crime to be an entrepreneur in China. It was politically incorrect to be an innovator. The only entity which held any wealth was the state. Today, it is a society of ever-increasing industry, productivity, wealth creation, and innovation. Whatever we think about the societal or environmental results of this, we have to acknowledge that it is largely a change of a peaceful, voluntary nature.

How did this occur? The factors are many and to detail them would involve an analysis of China's recent history. However, in Deng Xaoiping, China had a leader who recognised the need for change.

It must have taken courage and conviction of an exceptional order to instigate such a radical and fundamental programme, and yet he managed to achieve it. Above all, Deng must have possessed amazing confidence in his own ability, given that the very existence of the party that brought him to power could have been threatened by such change.

At the same time, he was a visionary. He understood that radical change was the only way of sustaining the Communist party in China. Despite the huge changes that took place under his leadership, and the background resistance that he undoubtedly encountered, he was totally vindicated. The party is still in government, is still strong and influential, albeit no longer in stereotypical communist form.

The people of that vast nation adapted very fast indeed, basically because many of them were longing for change. They learned that if they were industrious they could make and spend money. Their new-found economic freedom allowed them to fulfil many of their desires.

41

Change of direction

Such economic development required not just a change of action, but also a change of belief. The Chinese had been educated into accepting that the state was omnipresent, all-powerful and the provider for all – the 'iron rice bowl' syndrome.

In a remarkably short period, those beliefs were completely dispelled. Hundreds of millions of people had to learn to stand on their own two feet. They did so with formidable application.

The Communist party also reinvented itself. It experimented, bringing the new system into play gradually, region by region. Essentially, it unleashed an army of agents for change. Bureaucrats encouraged sustainable change and discouraged some of the sharper practices that came with it.

Reform continues with the implementation of a proper tax system and a fairer legal system. Today, a country with a population of almost one and a half billion people continues to modernise at a speed and efficiency that is truly remarkable.

Having seen the level of success during the initial period of change, China's politicians have become some of the most experienced change facilitators and managers alive today. Early success continues to breed more change because it is increasingly being perceived as a good thing. Zhu Rongji, the former premier, was even more aggressive in instigating and creating change than his predecessors. He 'coached' on a scale never seen before. He led by example and he was a remarkable and highly popular leader of change.

How many companies would like to improve their performance and balance sheets over the next 30 years to just a fraction of the extent that China has improved its economy during the same period? What if all companies – or at least, yours – could mirror such success within a similar period. How might you achieve such success? What factors would apply to such radical change?

External events such as 9/11 demand change, but on a smaller, domestic scale there must be the personal will to change. Change has to come voluntarily from an individual, whether in their private life or in the course of their career. In order to keep pace with the times and to fend off competition, change in commerce and industry must continue constantly.

Change from the top

Change within an organisation is usually the result of inspired leadership that galvanises people into doing things differently in order to improve and to move forward. Because change is a permanently evolving feature of life, leaders have a critical need to embrace it and turn it to advantage through skilled and visionary management.

However, the self-assessment needed to effect this is not always sufficient in itself. Most of us lack the necessary objectivity. We go on using the same methods and actions because that is what we have always done. We are victims of habit.

This attitude means that change can only come about with outside influence. By becoming aware of the full parameters of a particular situation, we can find the path to change – a way through the woods without the trees getting in the way.

Provided it is delivered in an entirely non-judgemental way, we can all benefit from an outside analysis of our working methods. Curiously, this approach lowers our natural defences rather than raises them, and makes us much more amenable to new ideas.

Change is about using different options. We often say to ourselves: 'I wouldn't do that if I were him or her. I would do it differently.'

The fact that we are ourselves and not somebody else is exactly the point. Usually we do not see ourselves as other people see us. In respect of our own choices and options, we have less objectivity than we do about those available to others. In order to get the best out of change we need to seek out as many options, alternatives and solutions as possible. But, as creatures of habit, we are now entering uncharted territory.

Managing, motivating and pioneering change are among the primary art forms of leadership. It also requires consistency, example, vision and communication, as well as adaptability and flexibility. All these qualities are crucial in good leadership.

Confidence is the single most integral ingredient of successful change: to do things in a radically different way requires a huge amount of self-belief.

Commitment to change

It is the job of an executive coach to raise the confidence of a client without creating a false sense of pride. Change for the better does not come about unless there is a defined commitment, and that must be underpinned by well-founded confidence gained from a full understanding of the risk-to-reward ratio.

An analysis of the strengths, weaknesses, opportunities and occasionally the hazards wrought by change, can provide a client with the level of understanding needed to forge ahead. It can dispel the fears, both real and imaginary, that often make people reluctant to change. Because we are so resistant to the concept of change, it takes time to effect. When we acknowledge this, we see that change – coupled with consistency – is not an oxymoron. They not only belong together but are also complementary to each other.

One of the reasons why executive coaching programmes should be designed and executed over a period of time is to allow the idea of change to permeate through the client's mind and put down roots. We all need to feel comfortable with what we are doing. Therefore, it is rare that a break in habit happens overnight – even if events sometimes demand that it should. The change may be implemented, but the belief in the validity of that change will take time to grow.

Motivating change is always a challenge because human beings, on the whole, resist the concept of change until they understand the advantages it can bring. We are quick to embrace the technological revolution that continues to affect us because, most would argue, it makes many facets of life so much easier. We can accept change when it shows us a clear advantage.

When a company decides to re-engineer its working methods, or reinvent itself, such change invariably affects every person on the workforce, and it is essential to keep them well informed. Involving staff in the process makes them feel valued. It creates trust because it demonstrates that their views have been heard and considered.

Communicate change

It would be a Herculean task to seek the individual opinions of 10,000 employees. But it is not difficult to communicate to 10,000 employees the issues a company is facing and why change is needed. It simply requires the will to do it.

The outcome will be far more positive if they rest assured that their interests have been taken into account. But that takes management and leadership from the executives in charge.

People accept change far more readily if they have a sense of having participated in the planning, particularly if they can add their voice to it. Most of all, they need to see the advantages of change.

This can be difficult when, for example, a new system means fewer people doing more work. It can be traumatic if some of the workforce lose their jobs or are asked to relocate.

However, the companies whose management fails to move with the times and innovate are the ones that go bankrupt. When that happens, every person in the organisation loses their job. Thoughtful communication helps organisations accept even distressful change.

Because rival companies will constantly seek competitive advantage through change and innovation, it is vital to stay ahead in the race. Business is a cut-throat world, with no quarter given to those who lag behind. That can mean re-training, constant learning and using change to our best advantage.

Adaptability stops people from becoming stale or bored. We have all heard a multitude of other adjectives used by disgruntled or disenchanted employees to describe how they feel about their job.

The biggest single cause of failure to implement change effectively lies in a lack of communication. Even if every individual in the team has the ability to embrace change, we can expect to experience difficulties along the way. With an executive coach to help voice the questions that need to be answered about the process underway, the actual process of change is faster and more effective.

Crisis also creates change, and therein lurks a real danger. When the driving force is a nagging worry or headlong panic, new initiatives may not be well thought out, properly communicated or effectively managed. We fear the unknown. We worry that untried situations will challenge our power or take away our control. And naturally we are all wary of changes that will create more work and complicate our lives.

Yet, ironically, crisis is often a direct cause of someone having failed to change or having failed to recognise that change was necessary. The result is often a 'damned if you do and damned if you don't' situation. Crisis limits a person or an organisation's ability to manage change to best effect.

If we can adapt in advance of – or in preparation for – events, then we will avoid crises. Self-evidently, this is a far better option. But such preventive measures require that we seek out change all the time and meet it face to face on our own terms. Under such controlled circumstances, change at its best is almost always highly productive, profitable, and even enjoyable.

Instigators of change

The runaway leaders of business today are companies that instigate fresh ideas and channel these innovations. Think of Yahoo! Think of Google. They both embraced technological change and communicated the benefits to their customers. Think Virgin, internet banks, Ryanair, easyJet, and a whole host of other successful companies that took a new twist on traditional business models and, in the process, revolutionised entire industries.

Their ability to take the universally accepted way of doing things and then turn custom on its head is what made them so successful.

But complacency is a cruel companion. A hungry competitor is always crouching in the wings, ready to grab centre stage by taking change one step further. Once that happens, the original innovator is relegated to the rank of just another operator. It's a salutary lesson in the need to invest in change.

'If it ain't broke, don't fix it,' goes the old adage. In general this is sound advice, but it's only a question of time before 'it' becomes 'broke'. The secret is to recognise what needs fixing before it gets 'broke'.

Results tell us when change is needed. If the result of our work or the progress of our organisation is not what we expect, then change is imperative. No matter what the reason, if we are not getting what we want then we must change. As much as we like to believe that the responsibility lies elsewhere, the buck stops with us.

The responsibility of an executive coach is to help an individual or organisation decide where the blockage lies and what exactly needs to be fixed, so as to help the client effect the necessary change.

One of the key issues facing modern management is the need to justify the company's performance and balance sheet to stakeholders. It is a brave management team that admits to disappointment in its own results.

However, the growing demand for transparency means that we are seeing this more and more. Increasingly high-flying executives are prepared to hold up their hands and say *mea culpa*.

This need for objectivity comes as companies, markets and regulators demand a higher level of performance responsibility. It is no easy course of action, especially when there is no game plan to get back on track and recoup any losses, or if the excuses for poor performance are not sufficiently plausible.

Short change

Yet despite this mounting pressure on senior management, there is increasing resistance to paying third-party consultants. Given the relentless drive for growth and profits, this is understandable. After all, many firms will have wasted substantial sums in the past on ineffective consultants.

However, it is hard to understand why any firm would be reluctant to invest in the people who work for it, if by doing so they can perform better and help to make the company a success. It is only by facilitating change, or adopting better tools and techniques that people become better at what they do.

The big difference between a consultant and a good coach is that the coach will leave the client with a set of tools that can be used *ad infinitum*, even when the actual coaching sessions have become a distant memory. A coach can instigate enduring change in the person or people.

A consultant who re-engineers a production system has also created change. But he will not leave behind the unlocked toolbox that can be opened the next time the production system needs re-engineering.

Management teams today should ask themselves why they have

not invested in their employees when they readily spend thousands of pounds on corporate entertaining. Is there not an anomaly in laying out money on a two-hour cocktail party for clients when for the outlay of an executive coach the company can reap the benefit of increased production, better services, a happier workforce, and a keener competitive edge?

Understanding change

Pierre-Yves has run a highly successful textile company for the last 15 years. It has made him a multi-millionaire. He recognised that he needed to change his business to keep pace with altered market forces. He decided to expand the company's services and hire new people.

On one particular morning when we sat down together, he spoke of his deep-seated frustration. He felt the investment had not paid off. The company was making less money than previously and he was in a dilemma whether to continue down the same path. We took a long look at the issues involved.

Together we reviewed the way the company was working, the size of the client portfolio and the changes that he had instituted within the organisation. We looked at the revolution taking place in the market. We looked at the factors that lay behind his frustration and we established that the crucial part of the problem was fear. He worried that he had embarked on the wrong road and the business might fail as a consequence.

Then we assessed the risks. We established that he could reverse the overhead growth if it became obvious that it was not producing the required results. We agreed that the risk attached to the changes that he had instigated was low because, despite the increased overheads, the company had no leverage or cash-flow problems.

Together we looked at what might have happened if he had kept on running his business along the old lines. We realised that during the previous two years the marketplace had changed dramatically. Had he not abandoned the old model, the company would not have been sustainable and might well have ceased to exist.

Trusting change

As we went through this process, his fear and frustration evaporated. He started to talk far more positively, saying he knew now that what he had started was right and necessary.

We established that the company, in its new form, had a greater client base than before and had maintained revenues despite a 75% overall drop in market spend. Pierre-Yves told me that the business was perfectly positioned to benefit from the pending upturn in the sector.

Better yet, the new approach had, for the first time in the company's history, given it a fantastic reputation within the industry – and this in itself was resulting in important new business.

As we talked, Pierre-Yves started to realise the depth of his commitment to the changes he had made. He decided that what was now needed was to entrench the new approach and continue to invest in change to build on this new-found success.

Thanks to the changes that he had already implemented, and those that are now following on, his company is set to increase its profits by a multiple of five within 18 months.

When the sessions ended, he told me that he understood the process of change much better, and recognised the time it takes to show real benefit. He was also more aware of the need to display determination, commitment and confidence in order to inspire and encourage the rest of his team. He had the escape-hatch of knowing that if the results were not what he expected in 18 months' time, then he still had the option to reconsider. Suddenly change was his new best friend.

Many executives think they are actually quite good at recognising the need to change, and of course many are highly adept at it. That said, we all need help in any radical programme. We need to ask the relevant questions and must have the objectivity to reach the right conclusions. Just as crucially, we can benefit from an impartial sounding-board to help us make the best changes we can.

Pierre-Yves had started reforming his organisation himself before he had the benefit of coaching. He had begun because he recognised that things could not stay as they were.

Lack of belief

His problem was self-doubt – a lack of belief in the enormity of what he had undertaken. He was in danger of losing his confidence. He was unable, without support, to take a long hard look at what he had so far implemented in order to decide whether these changes were effective. Without help – in his case the support of an executive coach – he simply could not achieve that level of fresh perspective.

Most of us are exactly the same. Once he had carried out this in-depth intellectual audit of the change to date, the actions and decisions he needed to drive the company further forward became that much clearer.

The moral of that story is that before our first coaching session he already had all the answers deep within him. Pierre-Yves, like many successful business owners, knew more about his company and its market than anybody else.

What he lacked was the time, space, and the freedom to reflect on what he was doing and why. He needed distance to review the outcome, so that he could decide whether what he had first thought was right and necessary would continue that way.

He was having a 'wobble,' and from time to time we all have wobbles. Even the most successful people on the planet have wobbles, especially during the inevitable upheaval brought about by change.

A concerted foray into the unfamiliar can deter the most confident person. We all remember that tension we experienced at the start of a new job, or when we are facing new challenges, and can't grasp the right way to confront them.

This sort of experience can be expensive for a company. When another employee is hired or someone is promoted into a different role, the newcomer is expected to perform as quickly as possible. Acceptable periods of adjustment are becoming appreciably shorter and the demands of performance are always escalating.

Despite this, surprisingly few organisations help people through change to enable them to perform better or faster. This seems to me to be tantamount to shooting oneself in the foot. It is like asking for a field to be ploughed, but leaving the farm with the keys to the tractor still in your pocket.

It is entirely acceptable to have high performance expectations – even through periods of change – but only if the tools needed to meet those expectations are readily available.

The ultimate change

On both a professional and a personal level the biggest change anyone can experience is redundancy. Losing a job is an excruciating process. It can destroy confidence, isolate and debilitate. It is the type of change that we all, understandably, fear.

I have seen strong, powerful people who have already had remarkable success in their careers lose all self-esteem and confidence when they lose their jobs. Often they have lost their livelihoods through no fault of their own. The experience deals a negative psychological blow that makes it significantly more difficult for the victim to find new employment.

In my experience, companies also suffer severely as a result of this. I hear former executives from perfectly respectable organisations become fanatical critics of their late employers because of the poor way in which their redundancies were handled.

While I acknowledge that it is hard to justify the expense of helping a former employee manage such a significant level of change in their lives, I also believe that it is in the future interests of most organisations to manage the issue much better.

It is difficult for the person made redundant not to take it personally, even if they have lost their job as a result of a structural change that is not directly related to their performance. This can, and frequently does, engender a fierce and damaging attitude towards their employer. But this might not exist if the staff affected could understand the sea of change around them and the stark necessity for the organisation to swim in a fresh direction in order to survive – even if this results in the loss of jobs.

When one of the big UK banks found it necessary to make a significant number of people redundant, it went to great lengths to help those affected to adjust by assisting them in finding new jobs. Furthermore, it explained why the redundancies were inevitable.

The result was a lot of very healthy publicity about how well the process had been managed, including testimony, praise and thanks from those who had been made redundant.

This enhanced the bank's image with customers, with shareholders and with future potential employees. It was a remarkable example of transforming a difficult, painful situation into a positive one, and a great example of change management. It was also, from a human perspective, simply the right thing to do.

To some extent, change is like learning to ride a bicycle. Once we understand that it is not an action to be avoided, but a process with advantages that can be invigorating and profitable, we learn to seek it out and do it naturally. Like many other habits, once we get used to doing it, we can do it again and again. This is the sustainable element of change.

Executive coaching is the tool of such change. It can help make the process possible, valuable and painless. However, much depends upon the power of our beliefs. Let's take a look at what makes our minds tick.

Before you read on.....

Back to you. What does all of this mean in your world, in your job? Are you change-resistant or do you embrace and take control of change? Are you constantly looking for better options and more creative ways of doing things or are you a creature of habit who would prefer to maintain the status quo?

Reflect for a moment on how you approach change. Then think about someone you really admire. Imagine that they have had a bird's-eye view of your life and your professional responsibility. What would they advise you to do differently?

If you knew that you would not fail and if you had complete confidence in what you were doing, how would you approach things differently? What changes would you make in the way that you do your job, think about challenges or manage others?

Jot down all that comes to mind. Then ask yourself, 'What valid reasons stop me from doing these things?' If you can't find valid reasons not to change, what is your action plan and when will you activate it?

Who do you need to communicate with about your plan and your vision and when will you talk to them? What will be the advantages to you and to them from this change?

4

The Power of Our Beliefs

'There is nothing good or bad but thinking makes it so.'
William Shakespeare

Much of executive coaching revolves around the improvement of relationship management. Our ability to successfully manage sophisticated relationships often depends on our own behaviour and its effect on others. In turn, our behaviour is governed, subconsciously, by our beliefs. Thus, in order to achieve an improvement of performance in a client, coaching frequently needs to act as the catalyst for behavioural change.

In order to achieve this we need to investigate and understand our belief systems and how to manage them, because they have surprisingly significant effect on our lives and our performance in the workplace.

'I believe I can't' inevitably means 'I won't'. Whereas 'I believe I can' actually means 'I will'.

Sarah runs her finance department well. She is known to be incredibly smart at her job. As she arrived for a session she sat down in a huff and started to tell me how everyone around her was letting her down. What was the point of working in an environment that failed to fulfil her expectations and where she was surrounded by people who she felt did nothing but hinder her progress? Sarah totally believed that all this was someone else's fault.

I asked Sarah if she had ever felt like this before. 'Oh yes!' she said, and then went on with some zeal to tell me how she had felt like this in every job she had ever had. Each one had made her feel disappointed. As she got to the third example, she told me that she had taken the job knowing that she would be disappointed.

Suddenly she stopped talking and there was a long silence as she thought deeply. I waited. Finally she said: 'Suddenly, I'm not sure if other people really have been letting me down. Could it be that I expect that they will let me down and then make sure that they do?'

Sarah had just done a major audit of her belief that others always let her down – and she realised that her 'belief' was, in fact, not true. Rather, she had been letting herself down. From this point, she started to take responsibility for her actions, replacing the old belief that others always let her down with the new belief that she needed to trust and encourage those around her so that her expectations were met.

Do you have 'beliefs' about yourself that are not as helpful to you as they could be? Identify some of these and then imagine the absolute opposite. Rather than limiting you and the way in which you view the world, would these new 'beliefs' free you to do and achieve more, to feel better about life and other people?

How it adds up

For someone whose whole career has been based on finance I had, for a long time, a very strange belief. I thought that I was bad at mathematics. I must have learned to believe this very early on in my academic career, as I took and failed my maths GCE 'O' Level five times. One of my lasting memories of school is the dread I felt before every maths lesson.

Oddly, I never equated maths to business. Business to me was all about making money and I have always believed that making money is something I do well. Luckily, it never occurred to me that calculating profit margins, estimating returns on investment, using discount rates to understand net present values of cash flows and so on are, in fact, the practical use of mathematics. My career might have been very different had I discovered this earlier. Then, during my coaching training, I heard several statements that changed the way I thought.

The first was that there is no such person as a bad student, only bad teachers. I thought about that over and over again. The more I thought about it, the more I realised that it is true. Look at children and how they can learn, at a very early age, to speak several languages fluently. They have no idea they are doing something that many of us believe to be 'difficult'. They simply do it because they have to, or because it is 'normal' in the environment in which they live.

Speaking frankly

I also carried another belief from school into adulthood. I was good at French, and I liked speaking French, I thought it was fun. Therefore I believed that I was good at learning languages. When, at the age of 31, my work took me frequently to China, I realised I would find it far more enjoyable and my job would be a great deal easier if I could speak Mandarin. I enrolled on a part-time course and, in two years, learned to read, write and speak Mandarin. I simply believed I could do it.

My first French master must have been a good teacher; my first maths teacher must have lacked the skill to awaken dormant ability in a seemingly slow pupil. The point is this: I understood that to get better results I needed to audit my beliefs. So I took a long hard look at the beliefs I held and whether or not they were accurate.

As my mind filtered this information, I came to believe that I could do almost anything if I believed I could. Obviously, I do not believe that I can fly and even if I did believe it, I could not do so unassisted. The point is that within reasonable, practical limitations that philosophy applies to us all. Every one of us can do pretty much anything that someone else can do. It only takes real conviction in our belief that we are capable of doing it.

Fear of discovery

'When am I going to be found out?' asks the worried executive of both himself and his executive coach. Sounds familiar? Chairman or sales manager, the gremlin of self-doubt is always waiting in the wings, ready at any moment of mental weakness to savage all of us, regardless of how far up the ladder we have climbed.

Much executive coaching is about eliminating negative beliefs and replacing them with positive ones. This is the process of raising a client's perceptions from their subconscious to their conscious and encouraging them to examine whether a particular belief, instilled in them in the past, is still relevant when applied to their present circumstances.

I was asked by a major financial institution to do an advanced numeracy test. In the past that would have terrified me, and the belief that I would fail would have guaranteed failure. I determined that if others could do well at such a test, then so could I. That may sound trite, but it is the truth.

I bought some books on how to pass such tests and set about practising, with an open mind and the belief that I could learn to succeed. Sure enough, as I practised, I got better and even started to enjoy the questions. On the day of the test, I passed with flying colours – not bad for someone who never passed maths at GCE 'O' level. The difference in the result this time was dictated by my entrenched belief that I could do it.

Another idea that made me think differently was that our unconscious mind is benevolent. It does what it is told according to its own interpretation of historical events. It does this by replaying our original emotions and reactions of the time.

Slither shiver

Let's take the example of my own phobia of snakes. My mother also had the same phobia. As a child I once saw her turn the television off using a broom handle while shrieking with fear. The reason? She had found herself inadvertently watching a programme about grass snakes.

Ever since I witnessed this, I too have had a deep-seated fear of snakes. So much so that I am afraid to walk in Britain through long, frost-covered grass in the middle of winter in case there are snakes hiding in the undergrowth. Of course, I am aware that Britain is home to only one poisonous viper whose bite is rarely life-threatening.

Given that snakes in many parts of the world can be deadly, it makes sense to have a healthy respect for them. But I know that my phobia is wholly illogical. It is a recognised fact that most snakes are far more afraid of us than we are of them. In general, they only strike when they think they are in danger.

Had my mother calmly watched that television programme and said to me afterwards: 'Aren't those grass snakes beautiful? It's a shame they are so afraid of us that we rarely see them,' my subconscious mind would have formed a radically different opinion as to whether I need to fear snakes in the middle of a British winter. As it is, my subconscious mind did what it was told. It built an irrational fear of snakes.

The fact is that our subconscious mind makes the best choice for us that it can, based on the information that it has been fed. Without us being aware of it, our brain determines that we breathe, regulates our temperature, tells us if we are in danger, reminds us to rest and it is our biggest sexual muscle. Our unconscious is constantly handling a multitude of tasks to ensure our survival at all times.

However, we spend almost no time monitoring the activity of our subconscious, checking whether or not it is processing information in the correct way and to our maximum benefit.

System overload

Our conscious minds can only deal with a limited number of issues at any given time. It is often mentioned that the '7 plus-or-minus 2' rule applies to our conscious mind. This holds that most of us can only think of between 5 and 9 issues consciously at any given time. Any more than that and we suffer from system overload.

When this happens, our mind dismisses some issues in order to make space for others that appear more pressing. As a result, we tend to spend more time thinking about paying the credit card bill and the mortgage than planning our careers and prioritising actions in the workplace that would create desired results.

We should spend at least some of our time encouraging our 'voice inside' to work out where we want to be in our jobs, what we want our lives to be like in ten years time, how to achieve that and how to perform better in our jobs.

Coaching allows you access to your unconscious mind. It allows you the opportunity to audit it and separate into digestible chunks all the issues we face. It allows you to focus and resolve one item at a time. A good coach will always encourage a client to face the issues that they are least able to contemplate, or least inclined to spend time confronting and resolving.

One of the greatest assets of a coach is to help a client to carry out a mental reality check. Was my own belief that I could not do mathematics valid? Clearly not. Would I have continued to believe for the rest of my life that I was bad at maths had I not taken the time and had the benefit of a coach? Probably.

The vast majority of beliefs are formed between infancy and puberty. They become our drivers, our road map of life. We refer to them unwittingly and take major personal and professional decisions based on the beliefs that we have always held, irrespective of how useful or relevant they are in our current circumstances.

We created our beliefs because they were useful to us at a certain point in time, because we perceived them to be necessary or because they were, as in the case of my snake phobia, 'given' to us. However, beliefs that become outmoded or prevent us from achieving our full potential can have a severely negative impact on our lives.

They'll find me out

All professionals inevitably carry their beliefs into the workplace and use them with varying degrees of success to direct their careers. However, we also bring along beliefs that are not useful. Misconceptions can hinder our progress as professionals and prevent us from achieving the full potential of our ability.

The classic example of this is confidence. Almost every successful professional I have coached has expressed the fear that one day they will be 'found out'. They fear, regardless of the empirical evidence, that perhaps their success is a fluke or temporary and that it will somehow disappear one day and they will be left there standing naked.

For a professional with a 20-year track record of consistent success this is clearly an unfounded fear, a restraining belief. These people, when confronted with the evidence of their achievements, generally review that belief. They start to gain more confidence in their professional ability and as a consequence begin to enjoy what they do.

Quiet confidence should never be equated with arrogance, yet most of us are inclined to assume that the two are closely related. They are not. It can be highly beneficial to know with absolute certainty that you are good at what you do. It is simply a belief based on truth.

While some negative beliefs may once have been of assistance to us, when outgrown they can be positively harmful. However, since the subconscious is benevolent, we can also train ourselves, and others, to open our minds to become what we want to be. We have a remarkable tool within us that talks directly to our subconscious. It is our imagination.

Have you ever noticed that when we use our imagination to fuel our fear it works brilliantly? Terror of not being able to pay the bills gets many of us out of bed in the morning. Our secret dread of being 'found out' gets us to 'perform' every day. Sometimes, fear of what the boss might say if the firm is losing money, or the stock market reaction if the growth target is not met, drives us to hit the numbers.

Positive imagination

All of that has its uses. However, if our imagination works so convincingly in driving our fear, it can surely be used to just as good effect in driving us to reach our goals and to realise our ambitions. Living in fear is tiresome and wearing. I prefer to live in my dreams and know that thereby they will become my reality.

So, each of us has this amazing tool we call our imagination, which most of us are conditioned not to use to its full effect or even to trust. It can change our ability to perform and it can answer one of the most elusive questions of life: what do I actually want?

In our imagination, we have the ability to transform our dreams into a temporary reality. But is it really only temporary? The obvious answer is yes. But why should that be? It is because we are conditioned that way.

Any sportsperson will tell you that the ability to imagine or visualise is crucial to success. How the soccer player imagines he scores the goal is the key to actually slamming the ball into the back of the net. Imagination is part of the reality. Indeed, it is a vital part of the reality. Business performance is no different. It is merely that we executives are not coached in the same way as sports professionals.

For example, while I was writing this book, I frequently imagined how I would feel to see it sitting on a shelf or reviewed on Amazon.com. To me, that made completing the book a reality. My imagination was saying to my unconscious: 'You will finish this book and this is how it will feel when it is published.' I was willing a future event into a present reality. It was driving my ability to write because I could feel and see the result of my work in my head.

Of course, I could easily have opted for the reverse side of the coin. It takes only a little loosening of the rein on imagination to become overwhelmingly daunted by what I had untaken.

'How will you find the time? What on earth will you find to say? I don't think I can do it.' Most significantly of all, that 'voice' inside me would say: 'Your objective is impossible.' Instead of willing a future event into a present reality I would be looking from the present into a yawning chasm of procrastination and failure called Some Distant Future. If I allowed myself that negative state of conscious mind, I would probably never have sat down at the computer and typed the first sentence.

However, by starting at the end of the process, imagining the book on a shelf, feeling the satisfaction and accomplishment of having finished it, writing it has been easy and enjoyable. My imagination told my subconscious I could do it and my unconscious mind obediently agreed and facilitated the work.

Executive coaching is a powerful way to unlock the imagination and assist executives to better manage the power of their subconscious.

Know what you want

Looking back on my career to date I am always amazed at how, as a young and aggressive executive, I used to go often into a meeting unaware of what I wanted from it. Therefore, I was unaware of how I would get what I wanted and often unable to know when I had been successful.

Today, I never go into a meeting without being well prepared. Just before it begins I take a few minutes to think about what I want to achieve. I visualise myself sitting around the table and reaching my aims. It is a highly effective technique.

First of all, I get what I want far more often than I did in the past. I also have a gauge by which to judge the progress of the meeting. I can check whether or not, at any stage, I feel the way I had imagined I would be feeling as the discussion continues. If I am not feeling that way, I know that I am doing something wrong and that I need to try another tack. Do it before your next meeting and see for yourself how effective the technique is.

The point is that my imagination, through visualisation, has created a belief that this meeting can be perfect. It tells me that I know what it feels like to be present at the perfect meeting and my imagination has created the belief that I can get what I want. The best part is that my meetings are now generally much shorter and more productive for all concerned.

One eternal constant

As we have seen in the previous chapter, change is the one eternal constant, and paving the way for change is a critical part of executive coaching. As we get older, our relationships alter and our professional responsibilities, capabilities and ambitions change. There is a constantly shifting undercurrent to all our lives – personal and professional. The workplace, in particular, is changing at a greater rate than ever before.

The nature of commercial success is rooted in the ability of companies to react rapidly to changing markets, customer preferences, the regulatory environment and umpteen other variables. Look at the changes in the airline industry alone. Pan Am, Swissair, and other long-established names in the aviation industry are long gone, whereas easyJet and Southwest Airlines are among the fastest growing companies in the world – thanks to revolutionary business models.

Such extremes are not confined to the notoriously volatile airline industry. Enron, the US energy trading company, and Arthur Anderson, one of the top accountancy firms, were also victims of change through the failure of senior executives. And we must not forget the dotcom bubble when many otherwise rational business and retail investors simply lost sight of reality, and cast aside all the basics of business.

Change is all around us and it is constant. Irrespective of age or education, every one of us has to grapple with the speed at which technology changes. We have to be tech-savvy simply to survive.

Modern life is like an accordion. Thirty years ago it was extended and contracted gently as the music flowed out at a reasonable tempo. Today, the accordionist is frantically pumping to make music at rave tempo.

Look ahead

Just how are we expected to see such change, embrace it and use it to our advantage in a commercial setting? Perhaps surprisingly, one answer is to take a little time out each month to consider what has changed, how it affects the way we work and the effect it has on our business, the market in which we operate and our stakeholder group. It is surprising how many senior executives easily lose sight of the big picture.

If we are not to become the victims of change we must ourselves change. We must move at the same speed as the change that surrounds us. For us to adapt as fast as our environment, we often need to be supported through such radical change.

I once had a client who was a 30-year-old bond trader. He had joined the bank for which he worked directly from university. In his entire career he had been managed by only two people and had never been in the position of managing others.

Then, unexpectedly, he found himself promoted to run part of the bank's proprietary trading operations. His job was to lead a team of five people, some of whom were his elders. My client had the power to make or lose millions of dollars for his bank. Suddenly, he was responsible, not only for his own profit and loss account, but also for the management of his team.

Effectively he had had no training to deal with this change of responsibility. However, our coaching sessions – arising fortuitously from a far-sighted managing director of the bank – were intense. As he told me later, they were also intensely useful in helping him to settle into his new job.

In the course of them, he learned how to cope with this new responsibility, how to effectively manage his team, how to handle credit risk and his profit and loss account.

He has since done very well. But I wonder how many people like him there are out there who were not offered the help of a coach to manage such enormous change. It makes me wonder how much money has been lost as a result of that kind of management oversight.

One of the stranger facets of change is that, in general, our beliefs do not keep up with our constantly evolving environment. A manager brought up by a father who always shouted at him is likely to lead his team by shouting at them. It is probably the only form of authoritarian communication and leadership he fully understands.

In most work environments today, bullying is not considered acceptable behaviour. Unless that manager is led to understand that it is better to be an inspirational and respected boss than a martinet, he is likely to lose his job or at least to reach a glass promotional ceiling. In such a case, it is not only the manager but also the company that suffers. It loses or caps the contribution of an otherwise valuable asset.

Mental breakout

Much of the skill of being a good coach is about helping a client to change, to embrace that change, to be able to see it coming and to be adaptable in their professional and personal lives. It is about developing new and better ways to perform and learning to break out from the natural instinct to do what we have always done. Change management allows a company to nurture and develop their most important asset: their employees. It allows companies to retain their best talent and to keep them performing at peak.

For the individual, being able to adapt to new challenges, technologies or responsibilities is an essential form of career protection. Only if someone can display their aptitude and ability to change will they be considered a valuable asset in an ever-changing world.

All of this is likely to require a change in our existing beliefs – something few, if any of us, are able to do unassisted.

Before you read on.....

Let's take a break for a moment and think about you and your beliefs.

If you knew that you could be an infinitely more effective person, happier and more successful, imagine what beliefs you would have. How would those beliefs be different to the ones that you currently have?

Which of your current beliefs do you think limit you from being the very best that you can be? Which ones were 'given' to you by someone else, by a teacher who told you that you 'could not' instead of encouraging you? Knowing that you can replace these negative beliefs, which positive ones would you put in their place?

Make a list of any of your current beliefs that you think limit you. Write down the opposite belief that you would like to have instead. Then consider whether or not you can accept the positive belief that you have just written down.

Think of examples in your own life, or the lives of people you know, where these positive beliefs bring obvious benefit. In the coming months evaluate in live situations the effectiveness of these new positive beliefs. Then review your list and decide which beliefs you want to adopt permanently.

5

What Talent Wants

'But what is happiness except the simple harmony
between man and the life he leads?'
Albert Camus

Most of us with professional responsibility today manage people in some capacity or other. Perhaps people report to you; perhaps you need to influence those around you; perhaps you need to manage your peers. Most of us have to manage our bosses.

Think for a moment of all the people that you manage in one way or another. Think of all the relationships that you have that require you to manage yourself or others to bring out the best in them. Think for a moment about how you like to be managed – or perhaps a better word is 'treated'.

Do you always consider how it might feel for those around you to be managed or led by you? Do you know what drives the people closest to you to do what they do? Do you offer respect, recognition and support as well as expect that behaviour in others?

Perhaps, you are involved in hiring people? Attracting, retaining and developing executive talent is a critical task for all organisations today. The vast majority of senior staff know that they do not just want to work – they also want to enjoy their lives to the full, both within and outside their work environment.

Therefore, time now has equivalent value to money, and there are other factors which are also important. All of us want a balance between our professional and our personal lives. We want flexibility. We want the freedom to exercise our judgement on when our

67

professional responsibilities need to take precedence over our personal interests – and *vice versa*.

People tend to be more productive when these two sides of their lives are balanced. Yet the higher a professional rises within an organisation, the more difficult he or she will find it to develop and maintain such harmony. Executive coaching is a critical tool with which to even our weight and position on the seesaw, thereby attracting and retaining the best talent.

We are all in search of that perfect balance in our lives that will result in happiness. In fact, all we have to do to achieve this is to make that philosophical shift from where we are now to where we want to be.

What is happiness?

The Concise Oxford Dictionary defines 'happy' as 'lucky, fortunate; contented with one's lot; glad or pleased'. Those few words describe a complex state of mind born from a confluence of events and emotions. But in reality, happiness is entirely subjective. It is primarily guided by circumstance, expectation and the comparison of our emotional situation to that of others.

We feel happy when we know that we are appreciated for who we are, or what we have done.

We reach a level of comfortable – even blissful – contentment when we are acknowledged by our peers to be successful in our personal and professional lives.

We are supremely happy when we feel loved, and when we feel love in return.

Reaching a financial objective can bring happiness, especially if that sets us apart from our peer group. For example, we feel happy when we can buy a bigger house or a more expensive car.

For most of us, the ultimate happiness and contentment is when we are surrounded by the people we truly care about. In an ideal world we would all be affluent and successful, with a wonderful romantic relationship and a number of close friends. We would be respected and appreciated in our work environment and enjoy our family to the full.

But real life is not like that for all of us, all of the time. Organisations play an increasingly familial role, providing a greater number of the components of happiness – components that in the past would have come from extended family, close-knit communities, or even religion.

It is not money as such, but financial security that for most of us plays a crucial role in contentment. Countless stories exist of people who have won lotteries and as a consequence became rich and miserable overnight. However, it is difficult to have peace of mind without financial security, even if we know that we will never actually be rich in the National Lottery definition of the term.

In today's affluent developed world, the majority of us are superficially a great deal better off than our grandparents. Britain's economy is twice the size it was 30 years ago, yet recent Government research suggests that we are actually no happier.

In America, incomes have trebled since 1945, but the proportion of people claiming to be happy has fallen. Another contemporary study in the City of London claimed that 80% of respondents to a survey on job satisfaction disliked their jobs so much that they would leave them if they could.

The evidence that economic growth alone does not lead to happiness led Lord Layard, Professor Emeritus at the London School of Economics, to conclude that measures to shorten the working week can be justified – simply because they make people happy.

However, we live in a highly competitive world where corporate and professional performance is judged by the ability to achieve continuous improvements in productivity, a greater return on capital and the creation of shareholder value. In that atmosphere, senior executives are unlikely to be able to take advantage of a shorter working week.

Money *per se* is a comparatively small component of our perception of happiness, yet this creates an opportunity and a challenge for employers. They need to reconcile the conflict between greater performance, higher job satisfaction and a better work/life balance – but without extra cost. There is an investment to be made here in executive coaching that can and will bring considerable returns.

Gruesome work environment

Traditionally, investment banks offer notoriously gruesome work environments. They tend to be pressurised, competitive, political money machines. When the money stops flowing, the axe starts falling. The hours and travel schedules are known to be some of the worst any professional can expect to endure.

If investment bankers were, for example, commercial airline pilots these working conditions would be illegal. However, the trade-off has always been the financial reward. Employees endure the endless hours and the impossibly tough regime because they have the potential to earn multi-million-dollar annual bonuses. Compensation packages are sometimes equivalent to the GDP of small countries. They also find themselves in a position to wield considerable personal power.

New entrants to investment banks throw themselves into their work and dream of the day when they will have earned enough to throw off the corporate yoke and embark on a more civilised life. But more often than not they burn out in the process. Thus talent frequently leaves at the first opportunity, and shareholders suffer as pay packages bulge in order to attract and retain talent. The irony is that this is not actually what that same talent wants.

The fact is that if they enjoy their work environment, talented people will be more productive and will work for less money. If they have a sense of belonging, they will feel respected and believe that their efforts are appreciated from on high. Money becomes a less motivating factor if they work in teams that accept mutual responsibility and interdependence, and that also permit an acceptable balance between their private lives and the demands of their careers.

When talented people work better and for less money, the returns to stakeholders are dramatically improved. Shareholder value is increased, clients get better results, and these employees have a much more harmonious work environment.

It is a truism that being around happy people makes you happy. The ultimate management tool is self-discipline born of a sense of group responsibility. This is backed up through the example provided by visionary leadership.

Few managers would deny that this is the perfect solution to harmony in the workplace, but the hard part is how to create such beneficial circumstances. What we first need to investigate is what makes people so discontented with their jobs and therefore harder to manage.

Lack of communication

It continues to surprise me how so many people can work in close proximity without having the slightest clue as to what they expect from each other.

They have no idea how they might be able to help, motivate or inspire each other. Few organisations spend time on proactively managing these critical team elements.

Many companies think they are doing all that is necessary when they set targets, hold off-site meetings and training sessions and send employees to conferences. But they spend remarkably little time communicating with the people within their organisation, helping them to manage colleagues and clients – or making sure that their senior staff know how to communicate effectively.

One overriding factor that makes people unhappy at work is if they cannot see the 'big picture'. They do not know how each of them fits into it and where their individual responsibility lies.

They resent not being consulted. When they receive regular personal feedback about what they do and how well they are performing, they feel so much more valued. This is absolutely not the same as an annual review of an employee which is carried out much more for the company's benefit than their own.

Too many companies treat their employees like mushrooms. They keep them in the dark and feed them on bullshit. What they need to do is to treat them like adults and communicate with them accordingly.

Employees dislike feeling powerless and lacking control over their professional destiny. In other words, executives at every level want to be treated as responsible and capable adults. They need to be helped to understand corporate objectives. But at the same time care needs be taken to make absolutely certain that they understand the exact role they are required to play within those objectives.

Invest in people

Companies spend immense sums of money communicating with their shareholders about their products and service – and even more communicating with their clients. Sadly, remarkably few do the same with their key assets – the people who work for them.

Why is it that a corporate hospitality event costing thousands is considered to be money better spent than the same sum invested in executive development?

While advertising and marketing budgets are necessarily large and important to the prosperity of many companies, would it not be wise to spend just 10% of those budgets each year making certain that all the employees understand the firm's aims and goals? Surely they would then all be able to pull in the same direction at the same time, and with real commitment to the job?

When the brief is made clear, executive coaching of individuals or teams can help corporations set clear expectations, communicate messages across the organisation and provide a valued work environment.

Large companies have vast budgets and expect to make enormous profits. Executive coaching takes up only a fraction of these to result in long-term returns that show up on the balance sheet to the benefit of shareholders. However, the real bonus comes from a revitalised and more contented staff that are sure of their role and aware of how much they are valued. I know from experience that such investments make a bigger contribution to a company's long-term success than almost any three-week national advertising campaign.

When I hold group coaching sessions with middle and lower managers I always begin by asking them: 'Why does this company exist?' Depending on what the company does they will reply with answers such as: 'To print newspapers' or 'To provide financial services'.

Then I point out that this is what the company does. But the reason that it exists is simply to make an acceptable return on capital for its shareholders. Very few middle or junior managers, and a frighteningly small number of senior people, give that reply immediately. Most only come up with the answer after significant prompting.

Rule of fear

Can the chairman of a global investment bank really believe that the people working below him are more productive, better at handling clients, and therefore more likely to produce profits, when they work 16 hours per day and have virtually no personal life? They are so tied to their desks that they take little or no exercise, and viciously compete with their colleagues for fear that the axe falls on their own neck next?

In such an atmosphere, the truly talented move on as soon as a better offer comes along. This endless process ensnares banks and similar companies in a salary spiral aimed at recruiting and retaining talent. The problem is that this practice ultimately reduces the return to shareholders and makes talent retention more difficult and expensive – the precise opposite to what the chairman is trying to achieve.

In a complex economic climate and amid vastly increased competition, it is essential for businesses to invest in their employees. They need to encourage and acknowledge their abilities, enhance their job satisfaction by providing a good working culture, and be aware of their overall needs as individuals.

This investment needs to be in both technical training and soft skill development. Better leadership and the ability to motivate others result in higher productivity, an enhanced atmosphere in the workplace, a raised sense of collective responsibility, and a corporate culture that nurtures and retains talent at reasonable cost.

It also results in lower stress levels and better employee health. It is a long-established fact that fewer sick days are taken by people who are happy in their work and have a greater sense of community.

I am a true believer in the philosophy of making money, but I also believe that more money will be made, both in the short and long term, only by investing in the 'people' factor. It is through this investment that organisations will achieve sustainable improvements for their stakeholders.

Knowing what we want

What do I want? Leaders, and indeed all managers of people, need to ask themselves this question and answer it with care.

Here are some possible answers:

- I want a company that is nimble, no matter how big.

- I want to keep good people.

- I want them to work hard and give 100 per cent.

- I want them to feel a sense of belonging and ownership.

- I want them to inspire and help each other to be better than good.

- I want a culture that replaces blame and 'can't' with inspiration and 'will'.

- I want creativity, plus the discipline required to reach and sustain peak performance.

- Most of all I want passion, good profits and long-term growth.

Next question: *How can get what I want?*

Pull or push

Most people work on the hope principle. This means that they are motivated by praise, appreciation, encouragement, support and enjoyment. This is the 'pull' factor, the proverbial carrot.

A far smaller proportion are motivated by the fear principle. This means that they will do whatever is required in order to avoid being yelled at. This may be because they are afraid of losing their job, or because they fear the consequences of not doing what they should. This is the 'push' factor, the stick.

Can senior executives get all that they want from their subordinates by using the 'push' factor? Of course they can't. Therefore, we should have no choice but to use blandishments. Let me give you a simple example of how this works.

Next time you are in a hotel and call room service, try listening to the person who answers the phone. If they tell you their name, use it.

Smile while talking to them and ask them how they are. Be human – you are not just communicating with a disembodied voice, there is a real person on the end of the line.

You will be amazed at the level of service you get. And you will feel good inside when you hang up. This is not because you know that your medium-rare burger is on the way, but because you will have made a friendly connection with a stranger. If you apply that principle on a broad scale you will get a significantly magnified result. It sounds too simple to be true, but it works. Every relationship in life is – or rather should be – a competition in spiritual generosity.

Rewards of recognition

Let me give you a real life example. I coached a board of directors in a hotel in Singapore. When I called room service and asked Angela, the room service operator, how she was, my clients in the room thought I was fooling around.

Indeed, they thought I was close to be being certifiable when I explained to Angela that we were working all day and that we would need her to help to keep us refreshed with coffee, iced water and the occasional bite.

When the waiter arrived, I welcomed him into the room by name, having checked his name badge as I opened the door. I gave him a big smile, thanked him profusely and told him that we had no money so we were unable to tip him. I asked him if he was OK with that. 'Sure,' he said, returning my smile.

Throughout the day, Angela made certain we had extra large pots of coffee and plates of Danish pastries. At one point she phoned to ask if she could send anything else up to us. The waiter breezed in and out, quietly serving us Angela's carefully prepared trays.

He got lots of thanks and no money. We all appreciated that both he and Angela were having a great day – they were enjoying their job and we were getting exemplary service. We all won.

As the session progressed, the directors talked about how they could employ the same blandishment principle with their senior managers. They in turn could use it with middle management, and once the idea took hold it could filter down through the organisation.

They decided there were some key points to remember in this strategy. What we first had to establish was exactly what we wanted: great service.

We agreed that the best way – the only effective way – to get it was to use the 'pull' factor. Angela understood why we needed her help, just as the company's managers needed to understand why their role was so important, and what was expected from them.

Like Angela and the waiter they needed to be told, by means of expressions of appreciation, that they were meeting those expectations. They needed to be able to exercise their own sense of responsibility.

Some people react better to the 'pull' factor than others and those people were identified to be used as 'energisers' within the organisation.

Once the directors adopted this approach and it was understood by the managers, it created a positive attitude which had remarkable effects on the company. As a result, even the recruitment criteria have changed. Today, an applicant's positive attitude is considered more important than their technical qualifications. The logic behind this is that it is easier to teach an employee technical skills than it is to engender a positive attitude.

Subsequently I was told that the 'pull' factor is now part of the corporate culture and has produced remarkable results at no cost other than example and a little time from the directors. They know what they want. They are getting it, and all members of the company are reaping the benefit.

The extra productivity means that they close the office earlier each day and staff have more time to enjoy their lives at home, or at least away from their place of work.

So congratulations, Angela. Thanks to you, 120 people across Asia are leading better personal and professional lives.

Antidote to the 'push' factor

If you work in a 'push' factor environment the natural reaction to someone being mean and nasty towards you is to play the same game back. Back-stabbing begets back-stabbing. The next time it happens to you, react in an entirely surprising way. Try KWK – kill with kindness. You'll be astonished by how such a simple, positive tactic takes the wind out of the sails of the good ship Bully.

Work/life balance is in large part directed by perspective. It's about the ability to discern what is important and what is not. The more stressed and frenetic a person becomes in their work, the less ability they have to differentiate between global objectives and day-to-day tasks.

The more an organisation focuses on internal politics, the less likely it is to reach its global objectives. Time spent on one-upmanship, ego and jockeying for position within the corporate pride is time wasted and money lost. However, to eliminate such waste everybody needs to be playing the same game. They all have to willingly adopt a culture born of the common good, as well as personal and group responsibility.

Aligning team perspective

Whenever I have trouble getting this point across to a big group of people within an organisation, I ask them a series of questions:

1. How old were you when you first discovered that it is more exciting to give rather than to receive the perfect present?

2. Do you feel better when you are helping someone else, or when you are receiving help from someone else?

3. How do you feel when someone asks you for help?

4. When someone asks you for help, what do you imagine they think about you?

The point is this: The vast majority of us feel better about ourselves when we are being positive and constructive, when we feel noble and proud, when we believe we are doing the 'right thing'. These are our conductors to happiness. They also make others happy. And when those around us are happy, we too tend to be happy.

Of course we all have bad days when we feel grumpy and we don't feel that we have the energy to give. But we get over those days far quicker when we have a proper perspective on our own situation, and if we work in an environment where it is hard to remain gloomy for long.

A psychiatrist can sometimes recommend that a patient suffering from depression should be given tasks that help someone else. The purpose is to direct the mind away from his or her own problems and increase feelings of self-worth by showing that such deeds can exert a positive force on another person's life. The effect of getting every single person in an organisation to do just one thing each day to help a colleague is quite amazing – try it yourself.

As individuals we all have choices and options, but too frequently we choose not to use them. Organisations work in just the same way.

Choosing to worry

We can decide to balance a successful professional life with a fulfilled personal life. The two are not mutually exclusive, no matter what your profession. We all worry. The question is, if we are so worried about a particular problem, why is it that we so often fail to do something about it? The reason is simply because we choose not to.

At the back of our minds, we all recognise that inaction makes the problem worse. It prolongs anxiety, and delays the solution. Yet as soon as we face up to it and start to act – even if it is not the right answer – it gives us a sense of proportion about the situation as opposed to a nagging worry that surrounds and consumes us. We have a choice – to worry, or to do.

If one course of action does not work, try another. Keep testing different options until you find one that does work. Choose to act in your own best interests – noting that this is different to acting in your own selfish interest.

Organisations and managers need to make the same choices and make those choices available to the people they manage. Executive coaching is a powerful way to bring these choices to executives, teams and whole organisations.

Before I discovered coaching I spent far too much of my life choosing to be unhappy or worried, and I now realise that it was all to no avail.

I have worried about losing my job or my home. I have fretted about being 'alone' or not having enough money. I have been haunted by fear of failure. I have brooded about losing people I love. I have even worried that, in comparative terms, I was far behind my peer group. I have allowed romances to make me unhappy.

I have chosen to think that my unhappiness was caused by others, and I have remained in a state of unhappiness for far longer than necessary.

In common with the rest of humanity, I have had expectations of life or of others that have remained unfulfilled. That has made me unhappy, even though these expectations were entirely self-made. On occasions, I have allowed my inability to accept people as they are, or events not of my making, to cause me great unhappiness.

Now I know that the more I accept people, events, and situations as they are and the fewer expectations I have, the happier I feel. I make a conscious effort to turn away from the 'if only' route: 'if only it were different.... if only I had got the New York job....'

Fewer things daunt me. The more I do, the better my mood. My worries become concerns that do not consume me. I get more done and I achieve more. My dreams are within my grasp. I have the energy to give. I help to motivate and I hope I also inspire. The more I give, the more I invigorate others and the more inspirational I can be.

It is a positive circle – one that you can choose to create for yourself and for others. For much of this, I have my own executive coach to thank, along with the training I have received as a coach. Both have made me sufficiently aware to make these choices.

So happiness is more than that definition contained in the Oxford English Dictionary. It is a state that constantly fluctuates, but above all it is about perspective and choice. It is about the right balance between life and work. It is about other people. And in the workplace it is about a corporate culture that acknowledges, embraces and feeds basic human needs.

Before you read on.....

I hope that this chapter has made you reflect deeply on some of your own 'operating systems'. Do you manage and lead others as you would wish to be led or managed? Do you set very clear expectations and help people, proactively, to achieve those expectations?

Let's do an exercise together. Using a flipchart if you have one or a pen and paper, write down a list of what you would like the people around you to think of you as a leader.

Create another column and write down what you think are the qualities of the leaders (or managers) who you most admire. In a third column, write down what you need to do differently to display the leadership qualities you most admire in others. Also state what you need to do differently to help others see you as the leader you want to be seen as.

Write down *when* you will start to do these things differently.

Make a list of all your worries. Then evaluate each worry individually. Consider for a moment whether or not each worry is in its correct perspective. Do any of them fall into the category of 'catastrophic fantasy'– in other words, are they either very unlikely to happen or totally out of your control? If they do, cross them off the list.

Next to each remaining worry, write down one action that you can take to start to solve the situation. Taking action – any action – is the key to shrinking each worry. Then write down when you will take that action.

Now consider how much better you feel and look at situations where you could use similar techniques to coach those around you in the same way.

6

The Toolbox

'If you never change your mind – why have one?'
Edward de Bono

Coaching is all about turning the natural way that we think upside down. There is much we can all do to coach ourselves and these are some of the tools and techniques that I, and many of my clients, have found invaluable.

This section is split in two. The first section explains those tools that you can use to coach yourself. The second section builds on these tools so that you can use them effectively to coach others.

1. Toolbox for self-coaching

The Trilogy Questions
- What do I want?
- How will I get it?
- When will I do what I know I need to do in order to get it?

These are questions that we ask ourselves all the time – so what is so remarkable about them? Well, the secret to their extraordinary collective power is to always use them sequentially and together on any subject. They provide a route-map to allow the objective to be established, the method of how to achieve the objective, a reality check on the viability of the outcome and an action plan with a time-frame.

The joy of these questions is that they can be applied to almost every single aspect of life – buying a house, getting a new job or promotion, drafting an email or simply a conversation with a friend. They can be asked about subjects both large and small. If any part of the three questions cannot be answered then that is a clear indication that more thought might be required before action is taken.

What do I want? I want to be rich and successful. So what do I want from this year? I want to earn 200k. So how can I earn 200k? Using the same questions you can progress from one goal to another, building layer upon layer of what I can do, one step at a time.

Using the Trilogy Questions before going into a meeting will keep you better focused on achieving what you want. Using them about how you will get what you want in your life will keep you working towards the goal.

Try them out on an issue that you are currently thinking about.

Know what you want from life?

We all seem to have a vague notion about what we want in life yet many of us find it hard to break it down into a succinct description.

And like any journey – it really helps to know where you are headed at the time when you set out. This next tool is designed to provide better clarity to the question that we all ask ourselves; what do I want from life? What's it all about?

The Nirvana Letter

My own coach used a fantastic technique on me, which I have since used to remarkable effect on each of my clients.

He asked me to imagine that I had suddenly jumped 30 years into my own future. Those two decades had passed in perfect harmony – they'd formed the central, career-building, accumulative phase of my life. What I had to do was to write to my best friend reflecting on what had happened to me during that period. I was asked to recount what I had achieved, what sort of life I had led, and to describe the professional and personal goals I had attained.

When I finished the letter that looked back at my life, I realised it had taken the form of a road map from the present to the future – but, of course, in reverse.

It clearly defined what is important to me and what core values I hold. It identified my positive and negative beliefs. From that vision of where I was in the future I understood, for the first time, clearly what I wanted in the present. I understood how that could be achieved, and exactly when I could get everything I wanted, and when I will know that I have got what I want.

I have been using that map with remarkable success ever since.

Looking back to the present, making the future real today, is the key to all coaching, turning the natural way of thinking upside down.

Many of us are not quite sure what we really want and, understandably, that can be a major obstacle to getting what we want.

For a number of reasons, this is an incredibly powerful exercise. Firstly, we are naturally accustomed to contemplating the future from the present. But this makes our dreams and desires appear distant, sometimes a little vague and unrealistic – and by consequence unattainable.

However, when you ask someone to imagine that their dreams have already become a reality by doing the dreaming in reverse – by imagining that future has already arrived, the wish list begins to have substance. The dreams have been fulfilled in the imagination and thus in our subconscious. That encourages us to regard them as achievable, engendering the great belief of I can = I will.

Since The Nirvana Letter requires the steps along the way to be identified, it becomes a genuine road map to the ideal future. It defines what we need to do in order to make our dreams come true. And it helps answer the most fundamental question in life: 'What do I want?'

Since imagination rather than memory is called into play, our thought process is not constricted by any of the normal barriers that the mind imposes when we think logically. These include that nagging inner voice that says: 'A house in St Tropez would be wonderful, but I know I'll never be able to afford one – so why bother to dream about it?' What is unquestionably true is that you are unlikely to get what you think you cannot get.

The written letter is also extremely useful, because it delineates the difference between what we have and what we seek. It indicates what we consider to be of value. It reveals what is important to us and so allows us to check that there is congruence between what we say we want and what our imagination shows that we want. It can be a very strong learning experience and one that often comes as a genuine surprise to the author.

When I first did this exercise it gave me clarity about who I am, what I want and what my values are – perhaps for the first time in my life. I had certainty about why I was working, what profession I wanted to be in, where I wanted to live and how I wanted to live. It was a revelation and a relief. I got pretty much everything I wanted within six months of writing it. That is extraordinary.

How to write the Nirvana Letter

Use your imagination to write to someone you totally trust. Write it from the vantage point of a number of years in the future: 10, 15 or 20 years hence – or even longer. Imagine that you are looking back to the present and that in the interim you have lived a perfect life. Keep this perfection within the bounds of reality. For example, if you have made £10 million 15 years from now, you have done so through work – and not by winning the lottery or receiving a legacy from a fairy godmother.

Start by describing where you are while writing the letter and the date in the future on which you are writing it. Then, as if you were counting backwards to the present, describe the events that led you to where you are. As you look back over your life to the present date, outline the major milestones you see.

Here is the letter I wrote. For the sake of privacy I have edited out some of the most personal parts but it gives an idea of the type of letter you might write.

Croix Val Mer,
France
9 November 2037

Darling Jo,

I am sitting overlooking the sea in Croix Val Mer. The sun is setting and the light has that wonderful limestone quality to it. The vegetation is greener now that summer is over but it feels autumnal, there is a slight chill in the air. The contrast that the light creates between the various colours has a certain harshness to it. It feels like a sunset at the end of a year, the end of an era, perhaps, even, the sunset of a life – mine. Oh, I am sure I will continue to enjoy this view for years to come, at least I certainly hope so, but sunsets have always made me reflective and this one makes me particularly so .

Do you realise we have now been friends for 54 years?! Thank you. You have always been more than I could ever have expected from a friend. You have loved and supported me through it all. Your energy, enthusiasm and laughter have been a constant inspiration. I know that were we having this conversation face to face you would now be protesting loudly that it is I who have been an unconditional friend and support for you. How wonderful is it that we should be able to disagree on such a happy subject. We have always said that you were born with all the right chemicals and, if I have the opportunity to come back to this world, I want the same mixture! In case I have not said it to you often enough; thank you. I love you.

Love. I suppose so much of our lives have revolved around this issue. I have always held the concept close to my heart and I am very lucky to have been loved and to have loved all my life. Love has so many forms, all equally valuable.

I was lucky to have been loved by my parents and to have the opportunity to love them in return both instinctively as a child and then consciously as an adult. I loved them, as you know, very deeply and I miss them to this day. Yet, I still feel them around me, or perhaps more accurately, within me.

As I write this I am crying more out of gratitude than loss. I think I actually did get the balance right between loving and caring for them and having my own life. I am glad I told them how much I loved them and that by the end of their days we loved each other unconditionally, with complete acceptance, warts and all. I continue to be proud of who they were, glad that they are so much a part of me. I think that as they look down on me tonight, they too are proud of me, the person they created, and I know they will be happy that I am happy.

I have also been lucky to have been loved by so many friends. People who are truly honest, whose hearts have been in the right place while firmly connected to their heads – a winning combination. To have been the recipient of such love carries enormous responsibility and I can honestly say there were few times when I failed to live up to that responsibility. Perhaps this proves that karma does exist, and that what you give is what you get or what you get is what you give. I don't think I know a single person who has had an 'easy' life. But life is easier when you can give and receive love. I will never forget the Christmas when I realized I was far more excited to see the faces of my family when I gave them the gifts I had so carefully selected than I was to know what lay wrapped up under the Christmas tree for me. I pity those who have lived long lives and never known that the greatest pleasure of all is to give, in all its forms.

And last, at least on the direct theme of love, is Kim. We have been each other's soul mate, lover and best friend for 31 years! How I despaired all those years ago of finding such a special person. I suppose I didn't help myself much in this respect until I moved back from Hong Kong, though I would not change those fantastic years there, even if I could. And then, out of the blue, came the most wonderful person to have walked this planet.

We have worked hard on our relationship and it has not always been easy. But as I look at Kim now, the two of us well past our prime, I am more in love than ever and I know it is reciprocated. You know, the only reason I would want to live forever is that I can't bear the thought of not being with Kim. Apart from being separated, I have no fear of death, just such gratitude for having had such a remarkable life.

Every human being is a unique blend of success, failure, joy and disappointment. I suppose that I slightly regret not fully knowing this to be true until I reached about forty. I am sure I would have had far less fear had I known and accepted it earlier. Needless fear, of others and of failure, limits one's ability more than any other factor in life; believe you can achieve something and, in most cases, you will. I am grateful to have lived by this philosophy for the second half of my life. It has paid handsome dividends.

We were in Shanghai last year. What a metropolis it has become since 1993, when I first tramped its bleak, damp streets filled with cyclists wearing Mao jackets! We went to 308 Plaza, the building in which we invested in 1997. It was an extraordinary feeling to look up at its 40 floors of gleaming glass knowing that it would not be there had I not sat in a hotel room for three solid days writing the feasibility study. If I had thought about it at the time I am sure that I would have said it was impossible. But I just did it. And now there is an amazing building that will survive far longer than me, perhaps for hundreds of years. Even if I alone know that it is a monument to the Tom Preston 'can-do' attitude, it is enough. Many people leave far less indelible marks on this world.

As I look back at my career, I feel amazingly privileged. It allowed me to live and work all over the world, meet some real characters, some of whom, were I to describe them, might be thought of as figments of a deranged imagination. I have seen many different cultures from the inside and built and maintained relationships spanning the globe. I may not have *made as much money as I would have done in a more conventional career, or one that had been more focused on the creation of wealth. However, I regard the experience as being as valuable, if not more valuable, than the money. Would I trade my experience for $20 million? Categorically: No.*

That said, how fortunate am I to be sitting here, now, with the sun disappearing below a blue grey horizon, knowing that Kim and I will be secure in whatever remains of our lives. We have the wonderful opportunity to spend time here in the South of France, to be at home in London when we feel like it and to know we will be cared for in old age and ill health – no matter what.

My career has also provided opportunities to make a valuable contribution to the lives of others. I suppose a good example of this is Glymen, the penniless, semi-starved tout we picked out of a crowd of hopeful and desperate taxi drivers at the airport in Accra when he had nothing. He drove us around that week, remember? Then at the end of it we gave him a job. To know he is growing old, content in his house with his wife, children and grandchildren, sustained by his total trust in God, is a wonderful feeling. I don't take sole credit. Much goes to you, Jo, and to the man himself but it is a small example of how we can all provide opportunities to people who then go on to use them in an ethical, honest and well considered way.

When I look back, I am awed by the twists and turns that led me into executive coaching. I still can't believe how lucky I was to find the career I love so much at the age of 40. You know, even now I can't give it up! I cannot think of a better way to earn a good living while helping others find the best in themselves, by getting the most out of their jobs and leading richer lives. It seems almost fantastical.

Thomas Preston & Associates is going from strength to strength with the 'young blood'. I am so proud of all the coaches and the back-up team. Can you believe that it is now attributed as being the best executive coaching firm in Europe? Quite amazing, and a tribute to the people and the power of coaching!

I suppose on the macro level my recent charity work for the homeless, 'Street to Home', is one of the things I am most proud of. It is the culmination of my values, my experience, and my wish to make a difference, plus my commercial acumen and management skills. To know that I began a self-sustaining organization that flourishes and has already helped countless people, is an achievement about which I am both humbled and proud.

Homelessness destroys. It is the developed world's most shameful humiliation. It is the cause of, or result of, some of humanity's most awful characteristics. If you were sleeping on a street would prostitution seem so degrading to you? Would heroin be a one-way street to death or a relief from reality? Would a Bentley be a symbol of what you can achieve or of what you despise? How must it be to feel safer on the street on a freezing January than with a husband who beats you and your children? And how often do we, the fortunate, think about these things?

Now, thanks to the work of so many, there is a realistic, if embryonic, solution for at least some of the people who suffer so profoundly. It is a judgment call as to whether these people have brought their troubles upon themselves and one I would rather not have to decide. We all make what we believe are the best decisions – albeit that others may regard them as totally misguided. But I have now seen many people turn their lives around and build futures that would not have otherwise existed. They then help others to do the same. I feel honoured and humbled because of my involvement in this. As the American philosopher Ralph Waldo Emerson wrote: 'To know that just one life has breathed easier because you have existed. This is to have succeeded.'

Well, darling Jo, as the sun goes down I am very fortunate to be able to reminisce in such a self-obsessed way but to a friend who is dear enough to wish to share in my innermost thoughts. How lucky I am to know you.

Tell me, how are things in Australia? And when are you coming to stay with us? You know you are always welcome and for as long as you want (or can bear it!). I miss you and can't wait to have you here in person so that we can bore Kim silly with all our African stories while we cackle like a couple of aged hyenas!

Come soon.

Much love,

Tom

Now over to you

So that is my letter. What revelations are in yours? Go back to the instructions above when you have a little time and write your own Nirvana Letter. Let your imagination open you up to the possibilities of all your potential, of all you are capable of being. Enjoy it.

Visualisation

What you have just done while writing your Nirvana Letter is a good example of the power of visualisation. It makes the future tangible and allows you to know what success will feel like in advance of it actually happening.

Visualisation is a wonderfully powerful tool for many situations, especially ones that require some sort of performance such as public speaking or job interviews. For example, a professional tennis player visualises each shot before he or she takes it. Long before the ball has crossed the net it lets them know whether the shot was a good one. They are able to do this by matching the way the visualisation 'felt' compared to the actual shot in reality.

We can use this technique to plan meetings, allocate time, create priorities and reach targets, and get ourselves into the right frame of mind before an important event. In fact, this ability to visualise on a small scale, say about a meeting, or on a big scale, about an entire career, can be one of the key differentiators between highly successful business people and those who are merely good operators.

In writing this book I visualised before I began. I imagined myself standing in a bookshop watching someone pick the completed work of a shelf, browse through it, and take it to the till. I wrote one chapter, and then I wrote another. With the completion of each chapter, that vision in the bookshop was drawing closer and closer. And here we are – in reality going through it together.

Another simple visual technique is to write a letter – in bereavement or at the end of a relationship that has not worked out. Write a letter to the person who is no longer part of your life. Express all the things that you would like say to them. And imagine them reading and understanding what you have written. More often than not this process eases the pain and helps to put the event into the past so that you can resume your life.

You can also use visualisation to push yourself to do things that you might be afraid of or that you feel unconfident about. Ask yourself the unusual question: if I knew I wouldn't fail, what would I do? Then act according to your answer.

Swapping shoes

Suppose you have a problem with a colleague, which is causing a breakdown in your ability to work together. Stand in a particular position and imagine your colleague standing opposite you. Describe to yourself what your colleague is wearing and tell the image of your colleague everything you are thinking about your working relationship together.

Then move to where the image of your colleague was standing and imagine that you are that person, looking back at the image of yourself. Now, from your colleague's perspective, say everything that you think that he or she would say on the same subject. This is usually a very revealing process in showing where the friction between the two lies.

Then go to a third position where you can view both images and think as a referee might between the two – make observations about what each of them could do to improve the situation between them. The net result is that you find yourself advising yourself on what you could do differently to make the situation better.

This may sound like tree-hugging but it can work really well. Just think how many times in conversation people have said to you: 'But put yourself in their shoes....'

A client explained to me that she felt bitterly let down by her boss. However, she hadn't told him how she felt, nor had she heard from him what she wanted to hear. I asked her to sit down and imagine him sitting over there. I then asked her to tell him what she was feeling. Then she moved over there, pictured herself as her boss and told 'herself' everything she wanted to hear from him.

Then she went into a third position and, as referee, gave advice to both parties. What she said to herself was: 'Anne, you've got to build a bridge with him and get on with life.'

Later that day she emailed me: 'I can't believe I feel so much better for having talked to an imaginary person out loud. Isn't that madness?' No it is not. The definition of madness is to do the same thing over and over again and expect a different result.

It's not crazy to talk aloud to yourself. But it is important how you choose to talk to yourself. How you talk to yourself is a choice. You can say I'm going to talk to myself in the way I normally talk to myself, or I am going to talk to myself today in a positive way. Actually, happiness and success are choices. If you're coaching yourself, make the proactive choice.

Role models

When you are unsure of the correct answer, take the ask-a-friend option. Mentally ask someone you admire to tackle the problem for you. It doesn't have to be an actual friend or even someone you have actually met – just a role model.

Suppose I'm having trouble deciding on whether to run the proposed office in Frankfurt as a wholly-owned subsidiary of the UK operation or as an independent company. What I decide at this stage may have a future bearing on our likely expansion into both the US and South East Asia.

Ask yourself what, say, Sir Richard Branson would do – if that's who you admire – or someone closer to home. Try thinking about the problem through the eyes of someone you respect. Putting yourself in other people's shoes is an important part of the process of change. If you are not getting the answers you want, proactively seek different ways.

The wheel of life

The wheel of life is basically your life split into sections. The outside of the circle is 100% satisfaction. The centre of the circle is zero satisfaction.

Draw a circle and divide the 'cake' of your life into equal slices representing professional satisfaction, personal satisfaction, financial satisfaction, work performance satisfaction, health and so on. You can adapt the cake and the 'flavour' of the slices to whatever suits best: it can be the Wheel of Work or The Wheel of Leadership or any other subject. Shade in each segment of the wheel to the level of satisfaction that you feel.

This is an easy way of gaining access to a client's views on a particular subject without saying: 'Do you think you are a good leader?' or 'Do you think you have a balanced life?' Filling in the slices requires a client to think about the individual categories of the whole. If the wheel isn't round, the car is going to wobble.

Worry

Worry is what drives most of us. It torments us through much of our lives, yet there's a very simple way to get rid of worry. Do something – anything – even if it's the wrong thing. The sense of motion stops the fear.

Imagine you are sinking under a mountain of credit card bills. You know that feeling, we have all been there, of being a rabbit caught in the beam of the headlights. We become frozen with inertia, despite the fact that lack of activity fuels the fear.

What could I do about this? Well, I could restructure the loan. I could call the credit card companies and ask for a repayment holiday. I can talk to my mother or my father. I can sell my house and pay off the debts. Investigate all the possibilities, choose the one that seems best and then act. At least you will stop worrying and you can always choose an alternative course of action at a later date.

Catastrophic fantasies

Just do *something*, don't sit there like the rabbit. Because that feeling of saying to yourself 'I am going to lose my home' acts as petrol on the flames of what quickly becomes a catastrophic fantasy that doesn't help. 'Where will I live? What will happen to my children? I'll go bankrupt, I'll lose my job....' Let's look at these misshapen phantoms of our nightmares.

'Oh my God, next year I am not going to have any business at all. The phone is not going to ring, emails won't arrive'. It is so very easy to quickly spiral down mentally to a point where negative fantasy takes over. Every single person has these irrational fears. What we have to learn to do is to pause, take stock of them, and ask ourselves if this is realistic. This time last year was I also having a catastrophic fantasy? Yes. What happened? I had a record year. So is it real to indulge in this catastrophic fantasy, or is it my mind that is playing tricks on me as part of nature's protection system? Dispelling fear is a critical self-coaching technique.

Pen-and-paper power

If you are worried about your personal finances, get the reality down on a piece of paper. Don't let the clouds of concern swirl around and obscure the picture. Separate mortgage payments, credit cards, whatever. Confront and attack each one individually.

The secret is to do *something*. Whether it is the right 'something' is largely immaterial. If it is wrong, you can always try another option. But you are going to feel quite differently – more positive – about the situation – because you have done something. If you are feeling positive, you are on track to solve the problem. Remember that there are always lots of options open to you – more than you can initially imagine. Never, ever stop at two. If there are two, there are four. If there are four.... keep going until you find the one that hits.

Write down what you are now going to that is different compared to what you used to do. Only by doing something different can you choose to think differently. By doing something different you made a choice and you will get different results.

If you do something and it doesn't work, do something else again. It's not hard. All it is doing is taking the whole electronic system of brain, mind emotions and resetting it. That's all it is.

Dump negatives

Get rid of emotional negatives. Too often we are invaded by that nasty little gremlin that nudges us into the rabbit position and turns on the headlights. 'I don't know what I want.... won't be able to get it anyway.... I won't get a pay rise because my boss hates me.... I'm unattractive to all women because I've just been dumped by my girlfriend.'

Write down on a piece of paper everything you're feeling about a negative emotion that you don't want to remain on board. Take the piece of paper to a safe place and burn it. You've shown yourself that you have chosen that negative emotion. You have singled it out and decided that you don't want it hanging around any longer. So get rid of it, physically.

Abandoning unwanted behaviour

'I should go for a long run this morning. I could go for a long run this morning. A run will help me lose weight. But, it's cold and I don't really want to. Actually, I can't be bothered to. I just don't have the time.'

You are in a place where you don't want to be, so it is normal to just try and bury the subject of the run. The solution is to go somewhere else: imagine how you feel from the standpoint of the run already having taken place.

95

'I did actually want to run, and I feel so much better physically and mentally for having run. I've structured my day around having run. I enjoyed it.'

The mental process can be applied to stopping doing something someone has become accustomed or even addicted to doing – like drugs or alcohol. What I want is actually what I don't want.

Intuition

For much of our academic careers we are trained to ignore or disregard our intuition. We all have this gift yet, as we become more familiar with logic and intelligence, we learn not to trust sixth sense and to use it less. But as I have already said, clients – indeed almost all of us – can instantly read the signals when something insincere is being said. Today we call it 'picking up the vibes'. It is a valuable trait in all of us and something we can and should trust.

There are times when we can clearly sense that somebody is telling us something that is not true. Our subconscious registers the tiny body language signs that other people display when they are not being wholly honest. We observe these giveaways without quite knowing how, but we make a note of them and that triggers a 'feeling' that helps us to interpret the signs.

It is often said, for example, that we can tell when someone is in love before they tell us, or that a woman is pregnant before anyone has heard the good news. We also get the same sort of feeling about places and buildings. It is quite a common experience to walk into someone's home and instinctively say that it has a good – or occasionally a bad – atmosphere. If asked to explain the scientific reasons for these reactions, we would be hard pressed to give any. We know, nonetheless, that we feel them strongly and that we are 'right'.

There are various levels of intuition. Sometimes, for example, you put down the phone knowing that both you and the caller have come away from the conversation feeling great. On other occasions you have a nagging feeling that something wasn't quite right. And nine times out of ten that feeling is 'spot on'. Trust it!

Similarly as a coach, when you know it is the right time to ask a client a certain question, do so without delay. It is almost certainly the perfect moment. Or when you suspect that an important part of a relationship with a client is not going as well as it should, you have probably guessed correctly. Explore your theory with the client.

My point is this: intuition does exist. It does work and, although not infallible, it is uncannily accurate much of the time. Use it; learn to listen to it and to trust it. Not only will this make you a better coach, the skill will sharpen as you grow more intuitive until it becomes one of your principal professional tools. It will also become an invaluable asset in your own life.

2. Toolbox for coaching others

If you are going to think like a coach, what mindset do you need to have? Firstly, you have to want to help that other person. Coaching is not about what you can get by changing the other person, or by helping to bring about change in that person; it's entirely about what he or she can get from it.

Secondly, you need to place yourself in a state of unconditional positive regard towards the person you are coaching. Let me explain. We are all very judgemental – we're hardwired to be judgemental. A precondition of good coaching is to accept that naturally, through Darwinian theory, we do the best we can to get the results that work best for us. That's just the way we are made.

What we don't always see is that we could improve on this in order to get more of what we want. But because we can't see the way to do that, we simply don't raise our game. Once you accept that someone is just doing the best that they know how, you stop being judgemental – and once you stop being judgemental, you have a whole different mindset about the person you are sitting with.

My job is to find a different set of tools that will work better to get what they want than the ones they are currently using. As soon as you have acquired that state of mind, you are over the hurdle. No matter who it is – within reason – you have real respect for the person you are sitting opposite. Purposefully, I have left my judgement outside that door before the beginning of the session.

If a client comes up with a solution that you don't think would work for you, it is crucial to remember that it doesn't have to work for *you* – it has to work for *him* or *her*. They have the answers, and you have to respect those answers. They may not be the right answer for you – but they know more about their life than you do. However, you can ask more questions and open up more options. They may think they have only two options, but there are an infinite number of options.

If I say to you, 'How are you going to get home from this meeting?' then, supposing that you came by train, you'll probably reply, 'By train'.

If I ask, 'Yes, but what other ways of getting home are open to you?' your immediate reply might be limited to 'underground or taxi'. But of course there are a whole range of options out there you are simply not prepared to consciously consider because they don't seem practical, but nevertheless they are still open to you: bus, coach, own car, rental car, asking your partner to pick you up, friend's car, horse, helicopter, cycle, motorbike, scooter.... and so on. One of the key skills of coaching someone is to help them come up with options they may not have considered.

Building rapport

This basic trust is the foundation stone for the rapport that the coach needs to develop for success, and this is a special skill. Given that most coaching sessions are for fixed and limited periods, he needs to build rapport rapidly. Sessions are hardly likely to be fruitful if the client is not at ease.

We all know instinctively when we are relaxed with someone and when they are comfortable with us. There comes a moment when we think: 'Okay, she likes me and I like her.' Often, we use other terms: 'having things in common' with someone, being 'like-minded' or 'on the same wavelength'. These phrases describe the process of becoming relaxed with each other, the process of building rapport.

Have you ever been in a restaurant where you have seen two people in animated conversation over dinner? They begin to look like as if they are part of a ballet. When one laughs, so does the other; when one drinks, the other follows suit; when one rests an elbow on the table, so does the other. And so it goes on. These are signs that the two people are 'in rapport'. They have obviously established good communication.

When you first meet a client it is possible to start building rapport with them by being 'similar' to them. One way to do this is by mirroring their behaviour, movements, position, speed and tone of voice – even occasionally using their own words back to them.

It is worth emphasising here that it is not the coach's job to build a two-way social friendship with the client. Indeed, the less the client knows about the coach the better. Any such information can interfere with the coach's basic role as a disembodied brain-partner for the duration of the coaching period.

Active listening

As a coach I listen, and I watch as much as listen. I don't just listen to the words and interpret them into my own language. Coaching is about listening to what the client is really saying. It's as much about watching and absorbing body language as it is about listening. Coaching is about giving your time and lending your brain as a thinking partner.

Distinctive indicators in behaviour provide the kind of data you can never gather on the telephone. If you suspect a client is not telling the truth even to himself, then you need these pointers.

We use the right hemisphere of the brain for construction, so turning the head to the right means the person is more likely to be telling you something that is not true. We use the left for memory, so turning the head to the left means we are reaching for recall. Of course, this partially depends on whether a person is left or right-handed. Our subconscious registers the tiny body language signs that other people display when they are not being wholly honest. It may be minute changes in skin colour, subtle eye movements or alterations in posture.

Where to begin

Start by asking the client to tell you a bit about himself. Always commence with open questions that have no right or wrong answers: 'Do you have any subject in particular that you wish to discuss?' This is a great question, because it allows the client to feel that he or she is in control and it offers a forum in which to raise the issues that are uppermost in their minds.

Format the client's subconscious by agreeing attainable goals for each session: 'I am going to achieve these three objectives today.'

If you are team coaching, make it clear that no-one, including the coach, is allowed to interrupt. Only when someone finishes speaking can another begin.

Everyone must agree that no assumptions are permitted. The enemy of communication is assumption. If you start to think you know what your colleagues or your partner want, you start to make massive assumptions.

A client states: 'My wife has a very expensive lifestyle and I have to work 18 hours a day to maintain it.' The assumption is that the wife wants him to do that. In fact, she may adopt the expensive lifestyle as recompense for the fact that she rarely sees him. She might prefer him to earn less money and spend more time at home.

Often the crux of a problem is revealed in an aside comment such as: 'I buy a lottery ticket, but I'll never win the lottery'.

But what makes you believe that you have less chance of winning than anyone else? It's statistically impossible, so what makes you believe that? In the throwaway lines lie the belief. So often the kernel of the problem is hidden in one of those asides.

Good questions, and plenty of them, are the key to successful coaching. The more questions a coach asks, the better they will understand the client. They will have an insight into the way he or she thinks, their values, beliefs, and anything that might prevent them from performing better at work and getting more of what they want from their personal lives.

I would also stress that good questions are born from genuine interest. Sincere and well-intentioned curiosity assists a coach to fully understand the situation and to get to the heart of it without jumping to conclusions. Questions frequently elicit solutions from clients. It is imperative, once the client decides on an action plan, to encourage them to put it into practice. The plan which decrees 'I will go and talk to my boss' lacks a crucial element – the time frame. Goal setting needs a fixed schedule.

The coach needs patience. The client may take three hours to come to a very simple solution that the coach saw two-and-a-half hours ago. But the client needs to get there their own way. The coach should not be in a hurry – which is why I do three-hour sessions instead of 40 minutes.

Suggestive questioning

I cannot stress enough the importance of open questions and good listening as the critical tools of good coaching. Although in 99% of cases coaching does not tell people what to do, it is sometimes necessary to lead a client towards what the coach thinks intuitively might be a good solution. By presenting this as a question, the client has the opportunity to reject it, if for some reason it does not fit with their thinking. In addition, by presenting a possible solution as a question, the client's subconscious, if it is open, will investigate the possibilities it offers. Phrased as an instruction or advice they will often reject it out of hand.

Let's look at some examples:

The coach thinks that the solution to a client's particular difficulty might be to talk to their boss about the problem.

Command: 'Talk to your boss'.

Since the mind almost always has a defensive attitude to suggestions coming from third parties the client is likely to think of a multitude of reasons why this should be rejected.

Suggestion: 'You should talk to your boss'.

The client is probably thinking: 'You may think I should, but you don't know....'

Suggestive question: 'Could you consider talking to your boss so that you can both find a solution to this issue?'

The client is likely to pick out certain words in that sentence. First, because it is a question, it requires thought. This is underlined by the fact that they are asked to consider an action. None of these words requires a defensive reaction. Then there is a suggestion that the boss might want to find a solution which would be in the interest of both parties. This set of words at least allows the client to override his default defence mechanisms to give the idea due thought.

This shows how powerful the use of particular words can be. With suggestive questioning you are leading your client, but always allowing them the opportunity to reject the idea. It is a very productive technique, especially if the client finds it hard to come up with options or solutions simply by responding to questions.

Back-tracking

This is the use of the client's own words by the coach. It works like this. The client says: 'When I think about how I can reach my sales targets I become anxious. I lose all concentration and I just feel overwhelmed by the task ahead of me'.

The untrained listener, hearing those words, will be seeking their own interpretation. They may respond with a different representational system to that of the client. Some people 'feel', some 'see' and others 'hear'. If the listener's representational system is visual, they may interpret what they have just heard as: 'So the client sees the targets as hard to reach, beyond their sight and too daunting to handle easily.'

If a coach uses his own representational system to repeat the client's words, the client will reply, 'No, that's not how I feel. I don't see the targets as hard to reach. I just feel anxious when I think about them and I feel overwhelmed'. At that point, the client will assume that the coach has not understood a word of the conversation.

If, on the other hand, the coach says: 'So, when you think about your sales targets you feel anxious. You are unable to concentrate and it makes you feel overwhelmed,' then the client's subconscious mind will respond: 'Yes, that's exactly it. This person really does understand me and what I am saying. They are just like me.' The client's mind is then open to the coach.

Therefore, the coach might follow up with a question such as: 'What do you think you need to do to reach your sales target?' Or: 'How would you feel if you did reach your sales target?' Once the client's mind is open and responsive it will then start to seek answers to the questions.

And remember

To coach other people you can use all the self-coaching tools you have acquired. Never ever coach someone who doesn't want to be coached. At the end of the day, remember that most people's ultimate barrier to success lies in not having the bottle to see if it works.

Before you read on.....

Think carefully how you will use all these tools that you now have at your disposal. Might you speak to yourself differently? Might you stop, think and then decide to resolve issues that are on your mind? And how might you use these techniques to enhance your relationships with others around you? Perhaps you will now do appraisals differently? Perhaps you will start to really build your confidence? Reflect carefully and make a commitment to yourself as to how you will think and communicate differently.

7

Individual Coaching

'What the mind of man can conceive and believe, it can achieve.'
Napoleon Hill

It is highly likely that you will be expected to coach people who work with and for you. Coaching today is a required management skill and one that is increasingly valued and talked about. Senior people are likely to have the privilege of being able to work with an external executive coach who will be specialised in talent development and encouragement of peak performance. However, the skills you are acquiring as an internal coach are of invaluable benefit to your staff, to your peers, and therefore to your company.

To employ these skills to their fullest extent you need to be able to exchange your managerial hat for your coaching cap. You need to make the mental transition of stepping outside yourself to act the same role as an external coach. For this reason, I would now be grateful if, when reading this chapter, you would think of yourself as that external coach coming into your organisation to coach.

Nervous?

I will never forget the first professional coaching session I did. I was nervous that I would forget all the techniques. I worried that I would not know what questions to ask. I feared that I would not be able to build any kind of rapport.

As my client walked into the reception all these fears magnified.

105

He was at the top of his game, confident, charming and full of talent. I wondered what on earth I could do to enhance this firecracker of an executive. We climbed into his convertible car and drove to the place where the coaching was to start.

During the journey I asked a few questions about what he felt about working for his company. Almost immediately he started to confide in me that he did not think highly of his CEO because he had not been promoted as fast as he felt he should have been.

I asked him whether his CEO was aware of his feelings and he said he thought he probably was. In essence, my client had been behaving in a way that only confirmed to his CEO that he had been right in not promoting him. As this realisation dawned on him he almost drove off the road.

The rest of the session proved to be incredibly useful for my client. He went away with a whole new perspective on his career – and I was flooded with relief.

So if you are nervous, don't be. Good questions and careful listening have a wonderful way of ensuring that any session will unfold naturally.

So, here we go

The most common form of executive coaching involves working with a single client on a one-to-one basis. Individual sessions can last between one hour and one day. In general, clients are successful individuals who are being groomed for higher office or they are already at the top of their profession.

I often ask them if they can recall the last time they were able to talk properly about themselves, their work, their issues and problems exclusively for hours at a time with a truly attentive listener. Most say that they have never had that opportunity. The concept, once absorbed, usually comes as a heartfelt relief. Without honest, objective and practical support while working at or near the top of an organisation can be a lonely and daunting experience.

The next step is for them to realise that the sole interest of the professional listener is to help them achieve greater performance in the workplace, improved all-round success, and a better life in general.

Executive coaching breaks down the barriers to success. Its primary purpose is to effectively and rapidly improve commercial performance and personal awareness. In its simplest form, it is to open up in a person a better set of options to deal with situations, events and people than those they have already used. It almost always revolves around some aspect of relationship management.

It applies in particular to the way in which an individual manages other people and to the way in which that same person manages their own behaviour and thought processes. A coach provides new perspectives and works solely in the interests of the client and their stakeholders.

During a coaching session, the focus is often on career progression. The idea is to establish the client's career goals, financial ambitions, promotional prospects, and to discover how best to manage their career. Much of this will be centred around the creation of profit, meeting the expectations of colleagues and stakeholders, as well as ensuring that a client has the technical abilities required to reach their goals.

The session will inevitably encompass romance and family matters, as well as other relevant issues involving health, friends, and personal finance. Although the primary aim of executive coaching is to improve performance in the work environment, it must equally address the holistic What, How and When questions to ensure that every aspect of the client's life is enhanced.

The coach is no fairy godmother who, with a wave of some corporate magic wand, can solve all of life's problems. It is the client – not the coach – who already has all the answers. The coach's job is to allow the client to find those answers within themselves.

The golden rule of executive coaching is 'question – don't instruct.'

That said, it is important to understand that there can be moments during a session where suggestive questioning may help a client achieve an outcome faster.

Absolute trust

For this to work, the client must have complete trust in the coach and accept that whatever passes between the two of them during the session will remain completely confidential. The coach will probably take notes. But these are simply an aide memoire. They will never be shown to anyone else. Any feedback to the employer from the coach must first be sanctioned by the client.

A coach....

- never tells a client what to do.
- never says what he or she thinks they should do.
- never imposes his or her own beliefs and values.
- never implies or passes criticism.
- never suggests that what the client considers to be important is either wrong or irrelevant.
- never tells a client how clever they are.
- never tells a client that they are foolish or inadequate.
- never reduces a client's confidence.
- never acts as a management consultant under another name.

The Trilogy Questions

For a session to be successful the coach must pose and the client must truthfully answer an interrelated set of three simple questions that are fundamental to coping with any issue in business and in life in general:

- What do I want?
- How will I get it?
- When will I do what I know I need to do in order to get what I want?

There is a familiar saying that the hardest thing in life is to know what you want. Once you know what you want, getting it is the easier part of the equation.

However, often we find it extremely difficult to define what we want from a business situation or from life itself. Our minds tend to float a fleet of options that represent things we might want.

By consistent use of questioning, delivered to both the conscious and unconscious mind in a way that prevents the mind from resisting or defending, a coach will unlock the true answer.

Take a look at this purposefully over-simplified example of how this works with an individual:

Client: My boss doesn't like me. I will not be promoted. So I hate my job.

Coach: What do you want?

Client: I want to enjoy my job and to be promoted.

Coach: How will you enjoy your job?

Client: By getting a promotion that leads to doing more interesting and fulfilling work.

Coach: How will you get a promotion?

Client: By performing according to my boss's expectations, doing a good job and gaining the respect and confidence of my boss.

Coach: When will you get a promotion?

Client: When I perform according to, or beyond, my boss's expectations.

Coach: Will you then have what you want?

Client: Yes! I will enjoy my job!

Coach: So what will you do now to get what you want?

Client: Focus on doing a great job and stop thinking that I am hard done by.

Coach: When will you start to do that?

Client: Now!

Executive coaching allows the client to confront a seemingly impossible question and then work – section by section – through the issues surrounding it, until this results in a solution and an action plan.

Even the example above, basic though it may be, gives a clue as to the power of that set of three remarkably simple questions.

'What do you want?' establishes the goal. **'How will you get it?'** shows the method to reach the goal. **'When will you do what you need to get what you want?'** provides a clear action plan.

It is important to acknowledge each goal attained because our tendency is to reach one target and then move immediately on to the next one, without proper acknowledgement of the first. This results in a sense of perpetual struggle, a lack of lasting achievement that can undermine our determination and confidence to reach another goal.

Too simplistic?

Is it really possible to ascribe to three very simple questions the power to positively change lives and improve executive performance? After all, these same questions crop up in everyday life with comparatively minimal effect.

The answer lies in the fact that the trilogy is rarely asked in the correct order, consistently or collectively.

When they are used sequentially and continuously, separating out the issues behind each step and breaking down the confusion surrounding the bigger question, they are remarkably powerful. Good coaching relies on these three fundamentals: What, How and When.

A coach needs to build a rapid rapport with his subject that is based on trust, complete confidentiality and unhindered communication. These are the foundation stones of the session and a skilful coach will swiftly lay course upon course of bricks on top, allowing the whole structure of the session to take a positive and ordered shape.

When the mind considers it is under attack, it employs a highly effective defence mechanism. In normal conversation it uses established patterns to make a choice, as this is an easier option than considering a new and better way of making a choice.

But when confronted by such a statement as 'But that is a ridiculous way of thinking!' its natural mechanism is to 'close'. It will actively resist the idea that there may be a better choice. Rapport, built properly, allows a coach to prevent the mind of a client from triggering its defence mechanism and encourages it to work to find a better choice or solution.

Check your baggage

In order to build rapport, the coach needs to park all his or her judgements and personal beliefs outside the gate before embarking on the relationship with the client. The coach must realise and respect the fact that the client already has beliefs that create their own reality.

His best choices are based on his own filters and values acquired through his individual experience of life. What has worked before will be used again, irrespective of whether it is still the best choice available. The client then implements actions and reactions moulded accordingly.

At the start of their relationship, the coach knows that by opening the door to his subject's benevolent subconscious he can allow access to a wider range of choices and better strategies. These can then be used by the client to getter better results.

A coach will also affirm that a client's beliefs are positive. He will establish that the goals sought by the client are practical, relevant, and fit into his or her reality.

In other words, the coach's job is to ensure that client achieves what he or she wants and what is in their own best interests and those of their organisation. Surprisingly, this is frequently not the way we act on our own. More often than not we are unable to be sufficiently objective about ourselves to realise that we are not making the best choices in our own best interests.

Good rapport allows the coach to 'speak' to the client's benevolent subconscious, often using the client's own language. This 'language' is by no means confined to the actual words used. The coach will absorb the manner and speed of speaking, body posture, breathing, eye movements, and other physiological evidence of the thought process.

The reason for this is that our subconscious prefers to be spoken to in terms with which it is entirely familiar. The more the coach imperceptibly mimics the client's own customised 'language', the more the client's subconscious is receptive. It believes, if you like, that it is dealing with a mirror image of itself.

These techniques are used right from the first instant of meeting a client and for the rest of the time coach and client work together.

The moment of rapport is reached when the coach can see, feel and hear the client's 'inner self'.

If you are watching two people from afar, you instinctively know how well they are getting on together. They tend to be in the same position. Their body language is open. They may be smiling or looking at each other directly. We ourselves are all aware of that feeling we get in a conversation or a relationship when we just 'know' that we are hitting it off. That's rapport.

Guide, don't lead

It becomes horribly obvious to the client when a coach is forcefully leading the discussion. A good coach will allow a client to set the agenda and then subtly guide the conversation thereafter. If rapport has not been properly established, it is remarkable to note how forcefully a client can resist a coach's attempts to lead a conversation. For the client this can result in a feeling of almost physical discomfort and frustration that negates any positive result from the session, no matter how good the intention of the coach.

Take a look at this scenario:

Client: 'I feel I am swamped. I find it difficult to prioritise and so I feel that I never get the satisfaction of starting and then finishing something.'

Bad coach: 'OK, I understand. You see all the things you need to do but you can't get them done. So what can you do about that?'

The coach has failed to use client's customised language. As a consequence the client immediately feels frustration that he has not been understood. Instead of focusing on an action plan he feels swamped. He feels compelled to try and explain again how he feels.

Now here's how a good coach might have replied:

'OK, I understand. You feel swamped. So what could you do to deal with that feeling?'

Through the familiarity of personal language, the client immediately accepts that the coach understands what he has said. He is now able to focus on the possibility of finding a solution.

It is very difficult for a coach to help a client without emotional co-operation. This is only achieved where communication between the two is open and positive without raising the barriers we create when we feel that we are being forced, misunderstood, judged or misinterpreted.

Boundaries

Having established good rapport and explored the territory, a coach may well discover that there are areas which the client is simply not prepared to discuss. Two reasons usually account for this closed attitude. Firstly, the client does not consider the area to be as important as the coach suspects it is. Secondly, the client has decided that, at this stage of coaching, this area of discussion should remain off limits.

It is true that it is the responsibility of a coach to encourage the client to confront subject matter they would rather avoid. However, it is also important to be immediately aware when a client displays active, conscious resistance to a topic – and not to cross boundaries uninvited.

With a deepening rapport, those borders will widen and may disappear altogether. At a later stage, when trust is sufficiently deep, a skilful coach can return to the same frontier post and enter the previously forbidden terrain without opposition from the client's mental border guards. However, it is important that a coach respects these boundaries and never tries to cross over without a visa.

I always begin a session by asking 'Is there anything you would like to discuss?' The question itself gives the client the impression that they have control, even if they do not have a primary point for discussion. Launching into a subject matter, decided unilaterally by the coach, can instil a defensive attitude in a client which will be hard to later break down.

If the coach makes the mistake of telling the client what to think or, worse, implying that what the client thinks is 'wrong', then the client's mind will immediately come up with all sorts of excuses to justify his entrenched viewpoints. This is useful to neither client nor coach.

Only when the coach questions the client's thinking in a completely non-judgemental way will the client explore better alternatives to reach his goals.

Operation MBI

My client Michael explained that he was involved, via a venture capital company, with a management buy-in (MBI). Michael stated that the managing director of the MBI target company was not aware of the venture capital company's intention to proceed with an aggressive acquisition strategy immediately after the buy-in was complete. Michael was stating this as fact and not as a situation that concerned him.

I could immediately see a significant number of dangerous issues arising in relation to this situation.

The first was that the acquisition strategy could dilute the equity stake my client was negotiating in the management buy-in – and this was my client's main motivation for being involved.

The second was the potential for an untenable working relationship with the MD when he discovered that his new colleague had not informed him about the acquisition strategy.

Thirdly, as a direct consequence, there was a distinct likelihood that a lack of trust would develop between the parties, fuelled by the possibility of a significant change to the MD's own equity holding as a result of dilution.

Finally, all this was likely to combine to make the relationship between Michael, the MD, and the venture capital company so fraught that the buy-in would not work.

Straying from the rule book

Sometimes the executive coach must be prepared to tear up a chapter of the rule book. I do not doubt that through a lengthy process of impartial – and then suggestive – questioning Michael could have reached his own conclusions as to the dangers of this scenario.

However, it was faster to point out the difficulties and to give him a range of technical and human remedies that would defuse a potentially explosive situation, and thus protect his financial and career objectives. These included building non-dilution clauses into the shareholders' agreement and suggesting that the venture capital company review its strategy with regard to withholding information from the MD.

It took only five minutes for Michael to grasp this and resolve to act on it. Furthermore, it transpired that he was unaware of such technical tools as non-dilution clauses, and therefore the whole matter could have had a very different outcome.

Most of the time a coach assists his or her client to find their own answers to issues. This is important because we tend to do far more of what we have decided for ourselves, compared to what we are told to do. Finding answers for yourself also facilitates long-term, sustainable changes in thinking and behaviour.

However, in dealing with hard business issues, it is extremely important for the coach – in appropriate circumstances – to be able to use instructional techniques to impart direct knowledge that may be of immediate help.

In addition, a coach may state outright a fear. For example, he can speak out if he feels that a client is in danger of losing their job or is breaking the law. After all, his loyalty is to the client and his or her employer.

A truly effective coach must seek to seamlessly 'morph' many coaching methodologies into a single power tool that uses the appropriate technique, at the right time, to best help the client.

It is also essential for the client and their organisation to appreciate that executive coaching is a finite process. While coaching relationships can last a long time, they must never turn into a dependency. Even when no longer being coached, the client should be able to fall back upon the techniques that the coach has encouraged them to learn. Hopefully, the client comes away from a series of coaching sessions with a tool box that will have a lifelong use.

Operation Africa

Richard had been asked to move to West Africa to set up a commodity trading operation. This was a tricky assignment as we had to create fictional business scenarios that might occur in the future. I had then to equip Richard with the best tools to deal with real events when they occurred in what, for him, would be an initially alien environment. I needed to pack a tool box of techniques for him to take on the voyage.

I knew he was going to face a wide range of difficult commercial situations. I also knew he was going to have to cope with all the multiple and perplexing difficulties of operating in a different culture. Further, because of the nature of commodity trading, many of his decisions would have to be made on the spot.

Richard was going to have to be highly organised and self-reliant. That required constant awareness of the objectives of the business. All this led back to the Trilogy Questions to provide a clear action plan: **What do I want?** establishes the goal. **How will I get it?** shows the method to reach the goal. **When will I do what I know I need to do to get what I want?** provides a clear action plan.

The first technique was visualisation. It is frequently the most effective way to establish not only what a client wants, but also how they will get what they want and when.

I asked Richard to imagine that it was the end of the first year of trading of the new operation. It had been a highly successful year, although there had been many challenges. I asked him to describe what it felt like to have achieved so much in a short period.

Once we had established the imagined outcome of the year, we started the process of investigating the individual steps that he had taken to achieve this success. What were the monthly milestones? What difficulties and challenges had he encountered? How were they overcome?

Using his imagination he answered all the questions. What we thus created was a road map for the first year of operation. We reviewed the proposed business plan and noted that the imagined milestones actually corresponded with the expectations of the business plan.

As we went through this process, Richard became more and more confident of performing within the expectations of the business plan. He felt capable of dealing with the challenges of such an awesome assignment. He became aware of the resources he required to be able to do the job properly and effectively.

When faced with significant change, a coach often needs to build the client's level of confidence needed to successfully adapt to the changes ahead.

I encouraged Richard to put aside some time each Monday morning to think about the week ahead. He then imagined that it was in fact Friday, and went through all the things that had been achieved during the week – when they had happened and how they had come about.

What this did was to give him both a structure and a timeline for the coming week. It made the required outcome for the days ahead clear in his mind. He reported that this technique allowed him to proactively control the week, achieving set goals as opposed to reactively managing and achieving random outcomes.

Richard then began to practise the same technique on a daily basis, imagining at the start of each morning the events and outcome of the day, visualising the various meetings that were due to take place and the tasks he needed to complete. He reported that, for the first time in his life, he was getting things done on time and in an orderly manner. It was, he said, a new experience in his commercial life to feel fully in control.

His overriding fear was being professionally alone in West Africa and constantly facing new business issues that he had no experience of handling. He was afraid he might make the wrong decisions and worried about the possible consequences.

He believed that he was capable of solving problems, since he already had a good track record on that issue. However, he was racked by fear that this ability might suddenly disappear.

To address this irrational worry, we took an imaginary problem related to foreign currency exchange. I asked Richard what he would do to solve the problem. He gave a perfectly logical answer. So, I asked, 'What else might you do?' He again gave a perfectly logical alternative answer. We repeated the process about 15 times.

Gradually it dawned on him that he could come up with multiple potential solutions to any one problem. The idea that there were many options available to any particular problem became established as a belief. Richard tells me he has since used this technique many times while actually on the job.

The Eureka! Moment

A good coach will do far more listening than talking. And a good coach really does listen – avidly. Active listening is a form of acute concentration on what client says and how they say it. It is a unique experience to be actively listened to, and it is an essential part of good coaching. Consistent and intensive questioning is a powerful technique to help clients achieve perspective.

The most rewarding part of any coaching session – for client and coach alike – comes when rapport and the combination of active listening and intensive questioning culminate in fresh perspective. It's the point when the client suddenly sees for the first time, not just the shape of the petals on the flower, but also the vivid colour of each petal. In my case I feel it in the hairs on the back of my neck. No coaching session is completely successful without my having this sensation. I call it the Eureka! Moment.

William came to me saying he was finding his job difficult. He was not motivated and was finding it very hard to meet the expectations of the particular sector of the armed forces with which he was working.

As the first coaching session got underway we discussed all the reasons that made William feel the way he did. As he talked, I sensed that none of those reasons were the real cause of the problem. To identify what was really going on, I needed to understand each part of his job so that I could know exactly what he did and where the problems might lie.

I listened actively and questioned. As we did this, it became obvious that there was a fundamental reason why the job was so difficult.

It turned out that William had never met his own client face-to-face. He had never been to the base to see the sector of the armed forces for which he was acting, and he had never had a direct discussion with the client to establish what was required. Three years into the job, both the client's organisation and William himself had failed to achieve the very basic step of getting to know and understand each other. They had just never thought about it.

When this became apparent as the root of the problem, William had a 'Eureka!' moment. At the next coaching session he reported on a visit to one of the bases. The meeting there had led to an agreed set of objectives between them and the methodology by which to meet those objectives. The clouds had parted. As remarkable and unlikely as the above sounds, it is the perfect example of how coaching can work.

Formula free

If someone came to you and said: 'Life is actually very simple. A successful, content and fulfilled life depends on the answers to a set of three questions. I can provide you with the three questions that can be applied to any topic in your life and I can enable you to find the appropriate answers' – how valuable would such a person be to you! Well, now you *have* the questions. They are the Trilogy Questions: What do you want? How will you get what you want? And when will you do what you know you need to do in order to get what you want?

That said, individual executive coaching is otherwise far from formulaic. The agenda and subjects discussed are set by the client. Subjects range from work/life balance through to defining leadership, team building, skill assessment and change management techniques.

This is the power of executive coaching – it is adaptable to individual strengths and weaknesses and therefore it benefits everyone with professional responsibility. It is entirely bespoke to every individual client in order to help that client perform better for their specific organisation.

Before you read on.....

Think of the people around you who could benefit from you coaching them. Think of how you would use the techniques such as the Nirvana Letter described in the previous chapter to help them break their own barriers to success.

Think about how you would like to be coached if you were them.

You may well be thinking that you couldn't possibly spare the time to coach the people around you. Well, let's consider what you would be doing and the effects of doing it. You would be giving the people around you the time to stop and think, to devise action plans that work, to accept the responsibility to take these plans and implement them.

Would this present investment in time save you considerable investment in time in the future? You will also be helping the person you coach – and therefore your organisation – to move more swiftly to success.

Make a list of the people you could offer to coach and how and when you would make time available to do so.

8

Team Coaching

*'Advice is like snow, the softer it falls...the deeper it
sinks into the mind.'*
Samuel Taylor Coleridge

The executive coaching skills and experience that you are now
gaining can be used as a management skill on both a one-to-one basis
and with teams. If you manage a team, think about how useful it
might be for you all to take a moment to stop and think about what
you are actually doing.

How often to do you step away from the coalface of e-mails,
phone calls and the rest of the daily workplace routine? Taking time
to consider how you could work better together and analysing your
business from a different perspective usually proves to be invaluable.
So what is the big picture? It's easy to lose sight of it.

And, as the manager of a team, ask yourself how much you listen
to the people who work with and for you?

Coaching a team requires exactly the same mindset as coaching
an individual. You need to step out of your role as a manager and
step into your role as a coach. Think about this and how you will
achieve it, because it is essential that you avoid falling into the trap
of 'telling' the team what to do. This is what managers, not coaches,
tend to do.

As you read through this chapter, I want you to see yourself as the
coach of your team and therefore to consider how you would conduct
a meeting with them as their coach.

Team coaching normally takes place over several months in either full or half-day sessions. These are spread equally across the agreed period to ensure that the positive effects are both embedded and sustainable.

Group (as opposed to individual) coaching is highly effective and every bit as productive. In many cases, since people rarely work entirely alone, it is useful to combine the two. This entails coaching one person over a defined period of time, while simultaneously coaching the people who work alongside him or her in a series of team sessions.

Why is this method so useful? The answer lies in group dynamics. When people work closely together they think they adopt a common aim. They assume that they share a mutual understanding. They think they have a common comprehension of their individual role within the team. Invariably, they believe they have a clear idea of their responsibility to the whole unit and what they can fairly expect in return.

Note that I say they 'think' or 'believe' that they grasp these issues. The fact is that in reality they almost never do.

More often than not, the views and understandings that they have are wrong, out of perspective, or not aligned with the perceptions of their colleagues. Usually they are nowhere near as closely aligned to their organisation's objectives as they need to be.

In one way, this is not surprising. We all filter and interpret information as best as we can, and inevitably we sometimes reach the wrong conclusions. By concentrating on the trees we lose sight of the immediate wood, let alone the overall forest. The greater goal gets obscured because of our natural instinct to see things as they apply to us individually, rather than as part of a team.

Once we have formed what appear to be logical conclusions about what our role is – or should be – we retain those images. It is only when things turn awkward that we start to question whether every member is singing from the same hymn sheet. When that proves not to be the case, Blame Culture tends to take control and destroy the ability of the group to produce results for the common good.

Dangerously, we make assumptions about fellow team members and then fail to test whether or not these assumptions are in fact accurate.

It is rare for people who work collectively to regularly audit their role and activities. Groups and teams require a facilitator from time to time to check that these remain effective. This is the role of the executive coach.

To illustrate the way groups and teams can lose focus, let us look at some case studies.

A major media company

Most of the directors had worked together for more than ten years. As a team they had achieved some remarkable successes, but an economic slow-down had resulted in a downturn in the company's share price. Surprisingly, despite 18 months of declining sales and reduced profits, they had been unable to agree on what action they should take to rectify the declining situation.

As business got more difficult, the group dynamics had deteriorated to such a degree that several members of the board were no longer speaking to each other. At a time when it was more important than ever to make informed and rational decisions based on shared information, effective communication had all but ceased.

Initially I had no idea that this breakdown in communication was so severe, but the severity of the situation swiftly became apparent. One of the great responsibilities of a coach is to scent and seek out any underlying problems and then encourage clients to address them in a positive way.

Before the first group session, I chatted to each member of the board individually by telephone to discuss what they hoped to gain from the coaching.

My main objective in doing this was to introduce myself and to lay the foundations of personal rapport with each of them. This was important because these private chats were to be followed up with a confidential questionnaire, which each member was required to complete.

I stressed that the strategy could only work if everyone was totally honest and frank in their answers. Any lack of frankness would be of little use to me and obviously of none at all to them.

Building a relationship

The telephone is a poor substitute for face-to-face coaching. What you can 'read' from a disembodied voice can only give you a broad-brush idea of what the underlying problems might be. I could glean only the barest of indications of the commercial issues the company was facing.

However, these initial conversations did provide some background knowledge and, most importantly, they provided the beginnings of a relationship based on trust.

I achieved this in three ways. Firstly, I actively listened very carefully to what each person had to say. Secondly, I managed to convince each of them of my genuine interest in bringing them all together once more. Thirdly, I managed to convince each of them that I was approaching their group problems with a totally open and non-judgmental attitude.

I then sent each member of the board the following letter and questionnaire, asking them to email me their answers no later than five days before the first scheduled coaching session.

Dear so-and-so,

I am writing to you with some questions that will be helpful in making sure the board coaching we are about to start is useful and productive.

Before we begin, please complete the questionnaire. When doing so, try to answer spontaneously with the first response that comes into your head. There is no right or wrong answer. Please do not show each other your answers. They are for my eyes only and will remain entirely confidential – even during the group sessions. Although you do not know me well, you have my word that all replies will be treated with the utmost discretion and confidentiality.

Please reply in bullet point form. The shorter and more concise the reply, the better.

Note that my job is to facilitate. It is not to judge or to provide answers. I am looking for the areas where you can improve what you do in your own interests – in addition to those of your company, your stakeholders, clients, suppliers, colleagues, staff and shareholders.

My intention is to identify old and obsolete habits, as well as patterns of behaviour and beliefs that limit or prevent you from getting the best from your own work and from those around you.

I want to ensure that you find alternatives that function better than the systems you use today. In other words, the object of the exercise is to bring about changes in working practice that will benefit every member of the board as individuals and will greatly improve the performance of your organisation.

My job is to ensure that you are fully aware of all the options available, not just your 'default' option which is born from years of doing things a specific way.

For this process to be successful, I need your help. Can you look on this as an opportunity? Can you be entirely honest? Can you be open-minded? Attitudes that don't help are: being defensive, justifying past actions, competitive criticism, or cynicism – in other words, all the negatives. If we avoid these traps, I know we are going to achieve great things and I am really looking forward to this!

The Questionnaire

About you:

a) What do you do really well?
b) What could you improve?
c) What aspects of your work to do you find easy and enjoyable?
d) What aspects of your work do you find difficult?
e) What do you most respect about your fellow board members?
f) What would you like to see them do differently?

g) What could you do to help them perform better?

h) What do you think your fellow board members think of you? (both 'positive' and 'negative' opinions).

i) What could you do differently to eliminate the 'negative'?

j) What do you imagine your staff think of you? ('positive' and 'negative').

k) What could you do differently to eliminate the 'negative'?

l) Think of a time at work when you felt truly motivated, inspired and at your best. What did it feel like? What did you look like? How did you sound? What was the effect on others?

m) What is the most important thing to you about what you do?

n) What is your ultimate objective?

o) What do you want from your work?

p) What would you most like to be different about the way the Group works?

About the company

In your opinion:

a) How does the market view your company?

b) How do your clients view your company?

c) How do your competitors view your company?

d) How do your clients view you as a representative of your company?

e) How do your competitors view you as a representative of your company?

f) How does your staff view your company?

g) How does your staff view you as a representative of your company?

h) What does your staff think that their role is in the company?

i) Do they understand the objectives of the company?

j) What is the ultimate objective of the company?

k) Which members of staff are most respected?

l) How well does the company communicate its overall objectives to its stakeholders, clients, suppliers, staff and shareholders?

m) What change in the culture of the company would best motivate all staff?

n) How can you communicate this change?

o) How do you communicate your profit objective to your staff?

p) How could you better communicate your profit objectives and the responsibility of each member of staff to reach those profits better?

q) If you were running the company alone, what changes would you make and why?

r) Please make note of any other points that you wish to raise.

Striving for harmony

The form is divided into two parts: questions that relate to the individual, and those that relate to the company and the role of the individual within the company. You will note that a number of them are repeated in both sections.

The purpose of this is to test the consistency of reply, to seek out areas where an individual's goals, expectations and beliefs are not aligned with those of the group. For a team to reach maximum effectiveness, everyone's personal aspirations need to be in harmony to the greatest degree possible.

Such unification can frequently be achieved by having each member understand how the team's overall success helps each of them to achieve their own aspirations.

The questionnaire is geared to remind the recipient of the broader commercial picture involved in managing an enterprise efficiently. The confidential answers provide the coach with raw data that he can feed back to the team to gain perspective on what they might do to improve the situation and how they can best do that.

It is also designed to focus the recipient on the strengths and abilities of their fellow team members that they may have forgotten. Each member is likely to have complementary, but not necessarily identical, skills and it reminds them that these assets can be available to the entire team.

The questionnaire requires the recipient to consider such important points of their fellow board members as 'what could I do to help them perform better?' This is important because most of us have a self-preservation system that runs along the lines of: 'I have tried, but I can't change things. It is not my fault.'

In fact, when the situation is not going so well, our responsibility to make every effort to improve matters is at its highest. We frequently fail to remind ourselves of this, opting instead for the route of least resistance.

At the same time, the actual physical process of filling in the questionnaire is designed to trigger a change in the attitude of team members. The questions themselves are designed to start the process of positive change.

The ability of each of them to consider matters from another standpoint will be crucial in helping to improve their effectiveness in the future.

In order to have reached the top of the corporate tree, members of a board are generally intelligent, capable people. Usually this means that their emotional quotient is at least equal to their intellectual quotient.

However, like the people below them, they can also easily lose perspective. This happens when they allow group politics – real or imagined – to cloud and colour issues. When open and frank communication becomes difficult, a person's powers of deduction are not always totally accurate or unbiased. He or she can put entirely the wrong interpretation on events or conversations.

The sausage factor

This situation compares with an old couple who have lived together for fifty years. One of them thinks that their partner doesn't like sausages and therefore never cooks them. The other thinks the reason they never have sausages is that their partner doesn't like them.

So, for half a century each of them thinks wistfully about sausages at breakfast on Sunday, but neither says anything to the other in order not to cause offence.

If that example seems to be a little unlikely, let me assure you that it is absolutely true. I was a witness to it one day when having breakfast with a married couple of friends. Not knowing that the subject was a 'no fly zone' I casually mentioned that I felt like having sausages. The husband said he rather fancied them too. Instantly, his wife retorted: 'But you hate sausages!' Her spouse replied: 'On the contrary, I love them. You're the one who hates them.'

Needless to say it was not long before all three of us were happily digesting the delicious forbidden fruit of fifty years.

The same miscommunication and misunderstanding, frequently born from good intent, is rife among groups and teams within the workplace and can seriously inhibit performance.

The questionnaire to the directors of the media company forked up plenty of 'sausages'. Over their ten years together they had developed some remarkably powerful barriers to communication. These fuelled whole platefuls of misunderstanding and resentment – with the inevitable result that the entire group had a seriously declining ability to effectively manage their business.

The team coaching process

Once the team coaching gets underway, with the entire board sitting in a room together, we used several methods to improve the group dynamics. Firstly, we posted three agreed objectives up on a whiteboard. I then posed a series of questions around what they considered were their greatest assets in running the business.

It did not take them long to reach the collective conclusion that, when they were working well together, they were each other's greatest assets.

It didn't take them much longer to agree that while there were some issues with which they could deal effectively, there were a whole range of others that were forbidden frontiers. They all felt too uncomfortable to discuss them in case they upset each other.

As a consequence, these issues had never been properly addressed and festered away like a running sore.

Very obviously, key aspects of the business desperately needed to change. Thus, the three agreed objectives posted up in front of them were almost impossible to attain.

Together, and in an open and positive way, we identified several of these forbidden areas and agreed to work through them.

All the board members acknowledged that in order to do this they needed to cast aside past prejudices. We dealt with some complex

129

issues relating to a magazine they had recently launched, on which they had hugely divergent views. It took a full three hours, but we reached consensus on what needed to be done.

We then agreed to explore the even more sensitive subject of their remuneration. However, before we began, we agreed to reach a resolution on the issue within half an hour – by using the same method and approach we had adopted to resolve the first issue. This we did.

In the course of the coaching, it became clear to each member of the board how much more effective they were when acting together and in a reasonable, honest and open-minded way. As the atmosphere lightened, the session became positively enjoyable. They were able to inspire each other and to rekindle the spirit that had moulded them into such an effective group in the first place.

In the following financial year, the company moved from significant loss to a very respectable profit. They did so by cutting costs, including their own fees, by 15%.

Positive team catalyst

It is essential that the coach acts as a catalyst of the positive within the group. For example, I usually ask each member of a team to tell the room what they most respect about the other members. When this is over, I can tell from their faces that all of them are dreading the next question. They assume they will have to spell out the qualities that they least respect about their fellows.

But this question never comes. Instead I ask each of them to state one thing about themselves that they could do better or differently to help the other members of the team. This reinforces the positives within the group and at the same time quietly reminds the individual of his or her responsibility to the other members of the team.

Another highly effective approach is to have each member state what is most important to them in their work – and what they feel is most lacking.

A design studio

The members of a design studio wanted to raise their creative ceiling. The issues discussed during the first meeting covered a diverse range of topics. They talked about recognition, freedom, encouragement, direction, constructive criticism, and fun.

This conveyed to the other members ways in which they could support their colleagues and help them achieve their personal best – and therefore the best for the team as a whole.

Motivation is an extremely important component of working with groups. The whole process is designed to exhilarate and inspire. This frequently involves reminding them of their success and the asset that they create as a whole and not as individuals. It also involves helping them recognise the many ways they can make working together rewarding, enjoyable and stimulating.

In the case of the design studio, the board of directors reported that the new and improved attitude of the team had been highly infectious and had spread through the entire company.

This came as no surprise. After all, if negativity and a 'can't do' mentality can permeate through an organisation, then positive thinking, a 'can-do' mentality and enthusiasm will be twice as infectious. These are attitudes that most people want to bring to their work, and therefore the whole team is far more receptive to 'catching' them.

Instilling positive attitude in a group, team or organisation is also a clear demonstration that a 'can-do' mentality and enthusiasm make the work environment more rewarding and enjoyable. That in turn produces better results at lower cost in terms of man hours, absenteeism, productivity and staff overheads.

During the team coaching process, the team leader is present purely as a participant and not as leader. This allows the person concerned to watch the dynamic of a team from a perspective that is never otherwise afforded them.

From this vantage point they are better equipped to see what both individuals and the team require from their leadership. It gives an insight into what he or she is doing well and in which areas they could improve. This usually comes as a complete eye-opener because they will be forced to reassess the preconceived ideas of their role.

It is for this reason that simultaneous coaching of the team, plus one-to-one sessions with the team leader, produce the best results.

Leadership is more often than not a lonely place in which to find yourself, but it can feel far less isolated after an exercise of this sort.

No place for a blame culture

We live, far too often, in a blame culture. One that accepts problems, actions and reactions as set in stone. All too often I hear people give 'I've never done that before' as the perfect reason for not doing it. They are ignoring the possibility that never having done it before may be the very reason for failure.

The investigation of alternative strategies, and the constant search for options that could provide the desired outcome, is a practice that the most successful business people use without even being aware of it.

Knowing there is most likely a solution to any issue if you search long enough is liberating. It means the individual or group is focused on future success, rather than being hamstrung by past failures.

Blame cultures are born when 'why?' is asked with no real intention to learn from the answer. Therefore, it is vital when coaching groups and teams to see that 'why?' is avoided in as far as it is humanly possible.

For example, a team may say: 'We just can't work as well together as we should.' A natural response to this would be to ask 'Why?' – thus creating and embedding the blame culture.

A more effective tool is to ask what the team wants to achieve. Usually they respond by saying they would like to be able to work better together. This allows the coach to move immediately to the solution by asking: 'What can you do to get what you want?'

The future is a clean slate, while the past is all too often a place where grudges, blame and misunderstanding existed.

Celebrate success

Just as in coaching individuals, praise born of genuine admiration is a powerful tool for group sessions. In fact, within a group it is often more powerful because of its force as a public statement shared and enjoyed by all members of the team.

However, the coach must always make absolutely sure that any praise proffered is utterly sincere. If praise is given in a disingenuous way, everyone in the room will clock this and the coach's credibility will instantly evaporate.

Again it is important that groups recognise that the coaching process concentrates on the three fundamental questions: What does the team want? How will they get it, and when will they do the things they need to do in order to get what they want?

Instant team coaching

If you wish to run a coaching session for your own team, here is a useful guide to how you can structure the sessions:

Rules

Lay out the ground rules up-front. No mobile phones, no hand-held internet access. A five-minute break in every hour makes sense for team and coach alike. Every member of the team must agree not to interrupt each other.

Agreed behaviour

Ask the team to agree a list of behaviours that they think would be useful for them to adopt, both during the meeting and beyond. Write the list on a flipchart and keep it displayed throughout the meeting.

Agree objectives

Ask the team to make a list of their objectives from the meeting. Once a full list is agreed, then prioritise the objectives so that you can address the most important ones first.

Where to begin

As the coach, work with the team through each objective one by one, encouraging people to share their ideas as to how the objectives can best be met.

It is often useful to share the Trilogy Questions with the team as a basic tool for producing a positive outcome for each of the objectives listed.

Before you read on.....

Think about how you would structure such a meeting with the team that you manage. Think about what pattern of behaviour you would like your team to agree upon. Reflect upon the most useful objectives that you could work through together. Most important of all, think about how you would act differently when being their coach rather than their manager.

9

Coaching Wealthy Families

'There is no wealth but life.'
John Ruskin

Hello again. You might be wondering what the purpose is of inviting you to consider the coaching of wealthy families. It is this: your skills are developing and your knowledge and understanding of how executive coaching works are now at a point where it is appropriate to ask you to consider how you might use these skills in specialist coaching situations.

If this challenge does not excite your interest, by all means move on to Chapter 10.

However, if you are curious, consider how you might address some of the following challenges and indeed, how you might use coaching techniques within your own family.

At the best of times, money – whether you are rich or poor – is a sensitive matter. Inheritance, in particular, tends to be a taboo subject. Many of us are brought up to talk about it all as little as possible. Too much talk about money is viewed as vulgar or ostentatious.

The majority of well-off parents want their children to enjoy a rounded upbringing that is not solely dictated by their fortunate circumstances. They want them to experience the camaraderie that exists between people sharing a common experience, such as school life or university, irrespective of their financial background.

However, for some, the enormity of their wealth and often their celebrity status cannot simply be ignored. The desire to bring children up as 'normal' members of society needs to be balanced against the pressures and responsibilities that befall those who stand to inherit large sums of money, considerable assets, as well as small or large corporations.

High net worth families have a special set of problems and concerns and therefore have particular coaching requirements. The coach has to deal with the whole subject of succession planning, as well as training the next generation to handle the huge responsibilities of considerable wealth. He or she also has to prepare them to take over and run successfully family-controlled companies.

Extreme sensitivity and complex dynamics often surround the various relationships within the family unit. A coach, as an independent third party, is in a unique position to facilitate discussion on these issues in a way that is completely objective.

Death and inheritance

The biggest issue the head of a wealthy family must address is that of their own mortality and the necessity for appropriate plans to ensure that the next generation is properly equipped to deal with their inheritance.

There are technical matters to be dealt with such as tax and trust planning, guardians, trustees, custodians and the fundamental need for a clear and indisputable will. While a coach cannot provide the expert advice required in those areas, he must be aware of the technicalities involved to ensure that the family receives the best possible advice from specialised professionals.

It always surprises me how many extremely wealthy families fail to confront these issues at an early stage. No family boasting generations of barristers would expect the next generation to be miraculously called to the Bar without first passing all the necessary law exams. Yet, frequently, those who inherit substantial wealth are suddenly expected to manage wealth and responsibility wisely without any training or experience.

Many wealthy families shrink from discussing the question of succession and inheritance. They often fear that doing so will burden their beneficiaries with a sense of being 'different'. They also worry

137

that foreknowledge of future wealth may cloud an otherwise 'normal' childhood and early life.

Frequently, rich families wish to instil in the next generation the work ethic as well as encouraging honesty, empathy and an understanding of the life that less fortunate people face. That is a wise approach. Few people are happy if they are trapped by their own wealth. Christina Onassis, daughter of the late Greek shipping tycoon, is a famous example of a tragic victim of gilded circumstance.

It is important that members of a family who stand to inherit substantial wealth do not become complacent about their need to work. They must be able to relate to the vast majority who are far less fortunate than them. It is equally important that they are not consumed either by the wish to hide their situation, thereby never being able to enjoy the privileges their circumstances can provide, or take the opposite course and ostentatiously flaunt their wealth and fritter it away.

Understanding wealth

It is useful for beneficiaries to be trained to understand the responsibility of major money and the problems involved in its management. They also need a clear understanding of their own situation, so they can hold true to their values and the things that are important to them individually, as against the impositions and demands that wealth can make.

To achieve all that requires a team effort by bankers, accountants, lawyers – and an executive coach.

Often it is the head of the family who tries to fulfil the role of mentor or coach. However, it is difficult for a parent to have the true objectivity and unconditional, positive regard required to see a son or daughter through the transition from carefree adolescent to responsible guardian of wealth.

I use the phrase 'guardian of wealth' specifically since in the context of many generations each new generation is simply a steward and temporary beneficiary of the family fortune, rather than the owner of it. The most successful families through several generations are those that understand and promote this sense of guardianship as opposed to ownership.

Very wealthy people often feel isolated and benefit more than most from the relationship of total trust that can be created with a good coach.

Everyone's needs and circumstances are different, so it is impossible to suggest a single, correct formula to follow in coaching high net worth families. Coaches have to have absolute respect for confidentiality in their work, regardless of the position or financial status of their client. But there are few more sensitive to the issue of confidentiality than high net worth individuals and their families. This sensitivity relates to all issues surrounding the family since many such people are, to a greater or lesser degree, subject to the public spotlight.

Let's look at a couple of case studies.

The Rossini family

This wealthy dynasty is of Italian origin. They have a manufacturing company with plants in Europe and Asia. The company is privately held through a series of trusts and is worth well in excess of US$200 million. In addition to the business, there are other assets most of which comprise real estate belonging directly to the family via various trusts.

The family has had extensive tax advice and is well structured in terms of financial affairs. The patriarch is a widower in his mid 70s who has, in the past year, started an intimate although not yet formal relationship with a widow in her early 60s. The widow has substantially fewer assets.

Two sons are joint heirs. Carlo is married with three children and runs the family business from Italy, for which he is paid a salary. Angelo, the second son, follows a successful independent career as an architect. He is currently not married and has no children. On the death of their father each stands to inherit 50% of the shares of the family business and a 50% beneficial ownership of all the other assets.

The business is such that, while it has significant and growing value, it also requires constant investment. Because of that, all the annual profits are reinvested in the business. The patriarch remains chairman of the company, but he leaves most of the day-to-day decisions to Carlo.

Secret fears

Both sons are concerned that their father's new girlfriend is more attracted by his money than his personality. In other words, they fear she is a gold-digger and that their father – at an age when his judgement could be clouded – may make a new will.

Carlo considers that running the family business is a labour of love because he pays himself below the market price for a managing director running an equivalent organisation. He thinks it is perfectly fair that his brother currently gets nothing from the business as he doesn't work in the business. He feels it is important to maintain the full portfolio of family assets, including the real estate dotted around the more desirable parts of the world, because he believes it will accumulate in value and will be enjoyed by his own children in years to come.

Angelo is deeply frustrated by all of this. He stands to inherit tens of millions of dollars – but only on paper. He will realise almost no tangible benefit because there is no cash. On his father's death he will still be required to work hard in his job as an architect. He will continue to live a comfortable, but not in any way privileged, life. He resents his brother constantly reinvesting the profits back into the family business instead of paying dividends.

He also feels that, since he has as yet no heirs and has made his brother's children the largest beneficiaries of his own will, he is entitled to more future financial freedom. This would give him the option to pursue his interests rather than be tied to his career simply to earn a living.

Angelo has tried to talk to both his father and his brother about these issues. His father ignores any attempts to discuss the subject and he believes this is because he does not want to be involved in any potentially contentious debates within the family. Angelo suspects him of trying to ignore the issue in the hope that it will be resolved when he is no longer around. Carlo simply will not contemplate entering into any discussion on the matter.

Pride and prejudices

Although he never said so, the father is of the opinion that he has built a family concern that can still compete in the modern business world. He is glad his eldest son decided to go into the business and thinks he is doing a good job. He takes the view that, because he has been frugal all his life, his sons should be the same, irrespective of the value of the family assets. He is inordinately proud of the fact that Angelo has made it in the world on his own, without financial help and without having to resort to the family business for employment.

The father is totally unaware of the growing resentment and potential friction brewing between his two sons. Moreover, he is enjoying his new romantic relationship and has decided to provide for his girlfriend in a new will to ensure that she will receive a comfortable but modest income from his estate on his death.

He has taken confidential legal advice and has been assured that, even if she were to try, the estate planning and system of trusts would prevent her from laying claim to any assets other than the income he intends to bequeath to her. He has not shared this intention with either of his children.

On all other matters, there are good inter-family relationships. At least once a year they spend time together at one of their houses and they see each other individually fairly frequently. In spite of this, the father and Carlo steadfastly avoid any conversations that might touch on contentious family issues. This adds to Angelo's growing frustration.

This is clearly a potentially disastrous situation that could lead to significant misunderstanding, discord and disruption to the family business at times when critical decisions need to be made.

The principal problem facing the trio is that they are unable to discuss the issues in a detached and unemotional manner. They have to find a way to put their various points of view across and to find compromises that meet everyone's needs and concerns.

There is such a communication blockage that each party, while having an inkling as to what each of the others is thinking, is speculating on the arguments they would make to defend their views. Thus none of them has a clear perspective on the issues, or the prospect of resolution or agreement.

Breakthrough

Angelo, whose firm of architects has benefited from executive coaching, asks a coach to facilitate a discussion between the three family members. Perhaps surprisingly, Carlo and their father both agree that this is a good idea.

It might seem that once everyone involved has agreed to engage a coach, the hardest part is over. We might assume that from then on the coaching would follow a similar format to that of coaching a group, albeit a group which is far more sensitive and emotionally charged. But because of the complex emotions involved there is a great gulf between family coaching and the coaching of a commercially-minded team bound by the structure and culture of a company.

In such a delicate situation as this, I find it useful to spend a considerable amount of time preparing with the individuals before gathering all the family members together. It is also vital that each member receives individual coaching in addition to discussions as a family.

This entails extensive time spent with each person separately identifying their key requirements, gently putting forward what might be alternative points of view, and investigating options, compromises and possible solutions.

Occasionally after these individual discussions, the coach may decide that feelings are running at such a fever pitch that any family meeting would be detrimental until further individual coaching has taken place.

It is also important to understand the way in which a family's wealth is structured in order to work out what options might be available. Sometimes a fairly obvious solution is not at all suitable when looked at in detail in accordance with existing trusts.

This means that it is frequently important for the coach to speak to family advisors: their principal lawyers, bankers, and accountants. However, a coach must never advise.

What can be achieved

Let's look at what the coach and the Rossini family can hope to achieve through following intensive one-to-one discussions and several family meetings:

1. Acceptance by both Carlo and Angelo that their father's new relationship is not a material threat to the family's wealth. This may in part, at least, reconcile them to the relationship.

2. The concerns of the children may have encouraged the father to take a closer look at the motives of the person with whom he is conducting the relationship.

3. Greater understanding by Angelo of the way the family's affairs are structured.

4. The adoption of a reasonable dividend policy by the family business. Alternatively, the appointment of Angelo to the board of the family business in return for a director's fee so that he can better understand the needs of the business. Alternatively, a review by an independent third party as to other possible methods of generating cash for the shareholders.

5. The disposal of the less significant properties. In this way both sons would have access to cash, while future generations are still able to enjoy the vast majority of the portfolio.

6. Mutual understanding by Carlo and Angelo as to the needs and priorities of the other.

7. The ability of the father to offer advice based on many years of experience and, at the same time, to recognise and understand the differing aspirations and concerns of his two sons.

8. The understanding by all parties that there is nothing that cannot be discussed so long as those involved approach talks in a positive, open-minded way.

9. A clear sense of guardianship of the family's assets for the benefit of future generations.

The Robinson family

The assets of this long-established British family are extensive and diverse. They include majority owned businesses, extensive financial investments, substantial real estate holdings and a complex financial structure that holds these assets together. However, over the years there have been some historical issues where and how the family's wealth is situated and invested.

Furthermore John and Simon, the current custodians of the wealth, form the third generation – often maligned as the one that loses substantial portions of a family's wealth.

Over the past five years the two brothers – both in their fifties – have had considerable trouble in managing the family's traditional business and have lost large sums of money in the process.

However, although the amounts involved are significant, the losses are fairly minor compared to the gains made by the family's portfolio of interests as a whole.

Of the two custodians, only John has children – a son and a daughter. It seems likely that only his daughter, Rebecca, has an interest in taking over the family business and the overall management of the family wealth. Max, the son is showing no interest in the core business and at this stage is pursuing a separate career.

John and his wife live in a large, but far from ostentatious, country house and they also have a three-bedroom flat in a fashionable part of London. Apart from exotic holidays in both summer and winter, the two children have been brought up in a conservative fashion. Their parents sent them to private schools, but took pains to ensure pocket money was limited to the level of their peers. Again, at university they were encouraged to follow a similar lifestyle to their fellow students and to work during the holidays.

Pressing issues

These are some of the issues facing the current custodians and their successors:

1. In a sense, Rebecca has been brought up too carefully – with too little exposure to the demands involved in preserving and

sustaining the family's wealth and assets. She is warm, bright, sociable and enthusiastic. Someone who makes friends easily. However, she has much to learn before she will be properly equipped to run the family's interests on her own.

2. She hopes to take over the core family business. However, the company is in a sunset business sector and therefore will require immediate major change to be viable in the future. Rebecca has only a vague idea of the sprawling assets of the family and the extent of the mantle she is assuming.

3. Her father, due to his tempestuous relationship with his own autocratic father, is wise enough to know that his daughter needs guidance from someone other than him at the start of her business career.

4. There is the obvious need to educate both Rebecca and Max on the detail of the structure and composition of their inheritance. This shared knowledge is vital.

5. There must always be a contingency plan in case illness or injury affects the heir opting to accept the leading wealth management role. In the interests of all concerned, this fall-back arrangement must ensure that the other heirs – in this case Max – can monitor the way the wealth is being managed.

6. Despite – or because of – the conservative upbringing of the children, there has been relatively little discussion among family members about their wealth.

7. There is a tacit assumption that Simon, the childless brother who shares current custodianship of the family's wealth, accepts that his niece and nephew will be the sole beneficiaries of his will. In fact, he and his wife are planning to make a substantial bequest to a cancer research body. The rest of the family is, thus far, unaware of this agreement.

8. This potential for disagreement demonstrates that there has been insufficient discussion between the members of the current

generation – about the management and about the planning involved in the administration of such a large fortune. As things stand, it is unlikely that custodianship can be transferred smoothly to the next generation.

When Simon finally revealed his intention to donate much of his fortune to charity, he agreed with his brother to bring in a coach to work with both generations on how the family business should proceed.

Coaching scenario

In a case like this, the ideal coaching programme is spread across a three-year period. Each quarter the coach meets with John and Simon for one day and with Rebecca for two days (with her brother Max, joining some of these sessions). The coach will also meet with the whole family as a group for one day.

In addition, the coach will also accompany them to some of the more important family business meetings and strategy meetings with financial advisors.

What is clear is that there are many issues facing high net worth families that need attention of both a technical and 'human' nature. The marriage of the two is often not as obvious as many would hope or like. It is also certain that, just like the preparation and training required in any job of immense responsibility, there is a long lead time of learning and adjustment. This should be managed before an individual or group is ready to accept and execute the responsibility of inheriting substantial wealth.

The issues facing the rich often depend on how long the wealth has been in the family. First generation wealth creators tend to be very strong characters with entrenched opinions put forward with force. They frequently have rigid views on what their offspring should do, how they should behave, and even what they should think.

Sometimes they have such high expectations that their children subjugate their own characters in order to meet the expectations of their parents. This can make it very difficult for heirs to develop their own personalities and establish their own values.

In a situation where the wealth creator wields strong influence, it can often be helpful for a coach to trigger discussion about the different values people have on their family's wealth. Inevitably there will be different views on how best to approach the management of money, and the management techniques that might be used by different generations to manage a family business.

This is particularly true when heirs are being groomed to take over a family business, and when the bulk of their commercial experience is gained from watching the style of the wealth creator.

There are many examples of entrepreneurs in the public eye who by dint of their strength of character will have trouble handing over their business reigns. These are the super-smart tycoons of the business world. The people who rise to the top and in the process do what most of us only dream of, by creating substantial personal wealth. However brilliant they are, these autocratic figures somehow find it hard to recognise when outside assistance could help them achieve their long term goal – to preserve and grow their accumulated wealth while enhancing their relationship with family and colleagues alike.

On the other hand, there are those who embrace the opportunity to make a seamless transition between generations. They spend some time and relatively little money ensuring that the family has the best possibility of long-term success. Along with lawyers, bankers and other financial advisors the executive coach can play an important role in passing the baton of responsibility from one generation to another.

Before you read on.....

Do any of these questions or situations apply within your own family? And if so, how will you address them?

10

You're a Professional!

*'We make a living by what we get. We make a life by
what we give.'*
Sir Winston Churchill

At this stage, you have acquired a broad base of skills and
techniques. However, it is the finer details that always differentiate
proficiency from professionalism.

Whether you are coaching people in your own organisation or
whether you intend to be an executive coach in a wider universe, it is
critical that you understand how to be completely professional. If
you are doing 'internal' coaching, this will help you to move from
the role of manager to that of coach.

Here are some insights into professional coaching practice.

Preparation

A good coach prepares for each session by reviewing the client's
details. I begin by reading a thorough job description and making
sure I understand what the client's managers and colleagues expect
from him or her. It is useful to have an informal chat with a client's
boss or other stakeholders in order to get an idea of the areas where
they think the client could improve. In a sense this is a mini 360-
degree review that helps me and the client become more aware of
their potential development areas.

This is also a useful process to ensure that the coaching taking
place is meeting both the needs of the client and also those of their

149

organisation. If agreed with all parties, I will share this feedback, carefully so that it is useful and an opportunity to learn, within the first or second session with a client.

I (or the client and I together) review it later to see if the client thinks they can derive the same benefit or if they have identified the same desired outcome or objectives as their company.

I see no conflict of interest in doing this, so long as the discussion with the company occurs before the coaching starts. In any event, I still keep an open mind when I meet the client and I am open to any difference of perception of development areas that the client may have compared to those of their organisation. However, before the start of the first session, it gives me a useful little insight into the direction in which the coaching might go.

A cautionary word here: it is not necessary to know the precise details of how someone does their work, and in fact it is often an advantage if a coach does not know. It is, however, important to understand the responsibilities of their job and the expectations placed on them by the people around them.

Where to coach

Wherever possible within the practicalities of corporate life, it is a good idea to coach in a neutral place, preferably outside the office and outside the client's home. This is because these areas are too familiar to the client and act as 'anchors' to entrenched beliefs and habits. A neutral environment helps to open the client's mind to new possibilities, options and solutions.

If I find that for practical reasons I have to coach in, say, a meeting room that my client uses frequently, I will change the layout before they arrive so it is less familiar to them. It may be something as simple as moving a table into a corner and positioning two chairs at right angles to each other for us to sit in. It helps if you can be seated in comfortable chairs, preferably in that position.

This opens up the space in front and encourages the client to think 'bigger' than they might when seated facing a coach. It also prevents the session from feeling like a business meeting where people usually sit opposite each other around a table. It is especially useful if there is a window with open views opposite the client. Again it encourages the mind to range further afield.

There are other essential factors in deciding where to conduct sessions in privacy. It must be somewhere your client does not fear being overheard. It has to be quiet so you can easily hear each other, and there must be no distractions. Obviously, a coaching session in a bar with a TV switched on will never work as both client and coach will be unable to fully concentrate on the job at hand.

Although sessions need to feel relaxed and comfortable, they also have to be in marked contrast to a social occasion, such as chatting to a friend. This is a professional relationship and it must feel like one to both parties.

I find hotel suites to be good venues in which to coach. Comfortable conference rooms often set the right tone, as do private rooms in restaurants. In the summer, I have also coached in parks, in a garden, and beside a swimming-pool. You can be flexible to a large degree, so long as the space fits the necessary criteria in a broad sense.

Confidentiality

Total trust between two individuals can take years to achieve and it can be broken in an instant. The contract between company and coach makes it absolutely clear that everything discussed between coach and the client will remain entirely confidential, irrespective of the fact that the client's company is paying the fee. This binding agreement is an integral and vital part of the coaching process.

If a client believes their coach is offering opinions, feedback or information gained from a session to a client's company, it hinders – if not entirely prevents – the creation of rapport based on total honesty and trust.

Obviously, if a client thinks, fears or believes that the coach is reporting back to the management, he or she will always try to give what they think is the 'right' answer as opposed to revealing the true situation. They will naturally shrink from expressing their real fears, beliefs, problems, issues and feelings. If this happens, it is more or less impossible for coaching to be of real value.

151

The one exception to the above is when the client wishes, and agrees in writing, that an aspect of the coaching – or all of it – be disclosed to the company. I believe that this is an option that should be available to the client.

I do, however, encourage the client to provide the company with a content-free critique of the coaching they receive. This may cover general issues as to whether the coaching has been useful in a corporate, business and personal sense. It may also include any measurable consequences as a result of coaching such as directly attributable improvements in profit and loss.

It is important for the company to be able to assess the effectiveness of the programme, especially since it will receive little other feedback apart from notification that a coaching session has taken place or that the contract has been completed.

Confidentiality is all-encompassing. It means not letting things 'slip', and never using to your own advantage the information to which you are privy – whatever the circumstances. Crucially, it means taking every precaution, be it with emails, phone calls or letters – in fact in any form of communication with a client – to make absolutely certain that there is no risk of an accidental breach of the rules.

From the start, a client must be assured that confidentiality is the primary concern of the coach, because it lies at the heart of their relationship. Confidentiality dictates, to a large degree, the level of trust and therefore communication between them. And only if there is truly open communication will the relationship be beneficial to either side.

Confidentiality is an enormous responsibility. If you know that you lack absolute discretion, or lack the ability to keep a secret, then in my view it is better to look for another more suitable career.

Note-taking and record-keeping

Note-taking in sessions is essential and this is an instant worry for the client. Inoculate against the virus of distrust before it strikes. From the beginning, in order to put them at ease, I always explain to a client why I am taking these private notes. It allows you to review the areas covered both during and after the sessions, as well as while the course progresses.

I find there are times when a client raises an issue without being prepared to discuss it further. When he or she shows this sort of resistance, it usually indicates a high level of importance. It is by and large a subject they are trying to avoid, and it usually ties into something else.

When this happens, I flag it in my notes as a reminder to go back to the issue at a point either when I feel they are ready to talk about it or when it ties into another issue.

I also encourage clients to take notes themselves. This is partly so that they keep a written record of their action plans and goal-setting commitments. It is also because I ask them to send me an email at the end of every session detailing what they got out of it. I ask them to do this, rather than me recapping in the next appointment, because it forces them to think back over the session at a later date, thereby reinforcing in their mind what it achieved.

I also ask them to use their notes to cross-check that they found what they said they wanted. It is another useful indication of whether the coaching programme corresponds to the wishes, needs and expectations of their bosses and colleagues. Finally, it shows where further discussion is necessary, and reminds me to revisit issues that may need further attention.

Of course, all these notes and emails contain sensitive information. This requires record-keeping that is meticulous and coded so that no-one could ever 'find' a file and refer it directly back to a particular client.

Trust

The implied contract between coach and client relies, above all, on trust.

'Trust *n.* firm belief that a person or thing may be relied upon; state of being relied upon; thing or person committed to one's care, resulting obligation; worthy, deserving of trust, reliable'.

Concise Oxford English Dictionary

Reading that definition, we may think we understand the meaning of trust. However, the premise of the definition is a 'firm belief'. Any trained coach therefore knows that, since all beliefs are entirely subjective, the definition is not as simple as it first appears. The establishment of trust takes time and must be fully understood between the coach and the client from the initial meeting.

The first point I stress to my clients is that *anything* they say to me will remain entirely confidential. A client will hear me make such a statement but they may not, at first, believe it. It is only as we build rapport that they will rely on me never to disclose to another human being what they have said and never to attribute what they have said to them in such a way as to enable a listener to identify them, in a case study or in any other way.

Key to the building of that crucial trust is that I do not judge the client, their actions, or thoughts or deeds. I start from the premise that whatever they are doing, saying or thinking is the best solution they have, or the best reaction they can give according to the circumstances they are in. Thus, if a client says to me, 'I get drunk every night,' whatever my personal beliefs on that issue, I will respond with a set of questions. I may reply: 'Okay, and what do you think causes you to do that?' or 'Do you find it a useful solution to the problem or a suitable reaction to the circumstance?'

Let me make it clear that I have absolutely no intention to encourage alcohol abuse. However, that 'judgment' or 'choice' is mine and not necessarily that of my client. Were I to say, 'Frankly, that's not a good idea – I don't think you should do that and I think you should give up drinking during the working week,' I would immediately destroy the rapport and honesty that exists between us and, in consequence, damage my ability to help the client. So being entirely non-judgemental is an integral part of the implied contract between us.

Obviously less extreme examples of this may be if a client is having marital problems, commercial relationship problems and so on.

I once coached an executive who came to see me under the guise of wishing to develop better concentration in the office. Some time into the coaching it became clear that the reason her mind was on other things was because she was consumed with the question of whether or not to marry her partner. I tried to investigate this in every possible way. Was it a negative belief about marriage? Was it a phobia about commitment? What were the client's thoughts about their partner? And so on.

I was getting nowhere despite the fact that the client, in true 'trust' mode had willingly divulged all their innermost thoughts on the subject.

As I contemplated this one day, it dawned on me that I had to use the rule that if one technique is not working, try another. Could it be that the client had built up the marriage question to such a degree that it, and it alone, was the stumbling block? At our next meeting, I suggested that my client consider getting engaged to see how it felt. I was not optimistic about this but the client – at first alarmed by the thought – started to weigh up the possibilities of this strategy and an hour later seemed to believe it was the answer.

The couple invited me to dinner to celebrate their engagement. At one point during the celebrations my client took me aside and asked me if I knew how excited they both felt about getting engaged, and how grateful they were for having had the opportunity to think differently about an issue that had previously seemed so difficult to resolve. The client also said that her work was going well again.

The duty of care

The duty of care demands that the coach, exclusively and at all times, considers only the interests of the client within the context of their organisation and personal situation. The coach must constantly try to bring out the best in the client. In other words, the coach must find out what the client wants and do everything possible to help that person to achieve their goals. The coach also has an obligation to protect the client's career at all times.

To the coach, the duty of care requires proper assessment of the course underway, careful consideration of the techniques and interventions to be used and constant monitoring of their effectiveness. Sometimes the duty of care even requires the coach to break some of the tenets of coaching. For example, there are times when I do feel it necessary to offer an opinion. In the past I have told clients of my concern that if they go on behaving in a particular way they may be at serious risk of losing their job. I do that only if breaking that most basic tenet of coaching appears to be in the interest of the client. In such a case, the coach has the responsibility to speak out, if no other alternative is available within an acceptable time frame.

The duty of care may also extend beyond the contracted coaching period. While it is important that the coaching relationship does not become one of dependence but rather one of empowerment and independence, it is also a relationship of trust and that trust cannot be breached. In this case, I refer to the relationship of trust in the sense that the coach can be relied on at all times.

Clients have frequently called me after the contracted coaching period with specific issues that they wish to discuss. I will always have reasonable time available in such cases. If, in my opinion, the time required by a client is becoming unreasonable, I then suggest another coaching contract for a specific period of time.

Rapport with a client is one of the tools that a coach uses to enter the client's mind in order to speak directly to the subconscious. It is incredibly effective but it places enormous responsibility on the coach to apply this with complete integrity and care. The client may not be aware that psychological techniques are being used during these sessions and therefore they must in all instances be applied with absolute integrity and care.

Respect

A coach needs to respect their client, particularly in relation to the boundaries that a client sets. To some degree this is connected to the requirement that a coach be entirely non-judgmental of their client. For example, the coach may suspect, intuitively, that a client is facing an issue that needs to be worked on, such as a negative belief. But it is vital to wait until the client raises the matter of their own volition or proves willing to discuss it. The client must never under any circumstances be pushed into talking about it against their will.

The coach's responsibility is to probe the issue, and sound out the client's awareness of the problem and willingness to discuss it without ever forcing the point. Respecting the client's boundaries is a subtle process done only in the interests of the client. No matter what the coach's view of the importance of pursuing the issue, that approach must be abandoned if the client is unusually resistant to any prompting.

There is one exception to this rule and that is when the coach is convinced that to avoid an issue could present an overt or imminent danger to the client's interests. For example, it is the only answer if the client's refusal to address the subject may result in the loss of their job. There are many subtle shades in the relationship between coach and client, and all of them are included in the implied contract.

Showing respect also includes simple courtesy such as arriving on time for meetings, and not cancelling except in real emergencies.

Honesty

It is essential that a coach is entirely honest about what they do know about and what they do not know about. Clients will pick up very quickly if a coach is 'faking' understanding of a project or the technicalities of some complex financial situation and this will inevitably damage the relationship.

No coach can be expected to have detailed expert knowledge of every subject that crops up in their daily work. Indeed, such detailed knowledge is not necessarily beneficial to the coaching process. However, it is paramount that a coach is qualified to recognise when a client's issue rests outside of their area of expertise and requires a referral to a qualified practitioner in a particular field.

Supervision

It is important that a coach has proper supervision. As we know, it is sometimes difficult to be entirely objective about ourselves, our own actions and behaviour. Being coached by another trained coach, or other suitably qualified professional, is an important part of ensuring the relationship between coach and client remains professional. It encourages the correct perspective, ensures best practice and allows a coach to ascertain that they have sufficient emotional and intellectual distance from their clients. It also helps flag potential problem areas should they arise and allows discussion as to how best to act in any situation.

In addition, a coach experiences exactly the same emotions and challenges as any other professional, so he or she needs the ability to seek all the advantages of coaching for themselves.

Because of the nature of the job, an executive coach can suffer from a sense of isolation in much the same way that many executives do. Most of their working life is spent being completely focused on clients and there can be times when it is both emotionally and mentally draining. Thus, having a properly trained coach or supervisor helps give coaches the support and the sympathetic ear that they, too, inevitably need.

Professional relationship

It must not be forgotten that the relationship between an executive coach and a client is entirely professional. This can be difficult, because, inevitably, as the relationship builds it can feel intensely personal. The client has probably never had anyone as totally focused on them and their thoughts, careers and lives as their coach. They are able to confide things that perhaps they would not tell anyone else in the world. Not even their spouses. The coach is totally 'there' for them and thinking entirely in their client's interests.

This can inevitably feel, to the client and potentially to the coach, rather more like a friendship. It is vital for both sides to recognise and remember that this as purely a professional interchange. It is not a personal relationship. It will not continue beyond a certain limit of time; it is a formal relationship with clear and distinct boundaries. The client must never be allowed to become dependent on a coach.

In my experience, a number of things help to keep the interplay between coach and client on the appropriate lines. I talk about myself, my life and the things that are important to me as little as common courtesy will allow with clients. I have an imaginary barrier in my mind that differentiates what I might say to my friends, for example, compared to my clients.

At the start of the coaching process, clients often want to know some basics about a coach's life, and I am happy to answer any questions they may have with total honesty. However, I am not being paid to talk about me, but about them.

I also find that it is helpful to put the relationship into perspective. I ensure that they know what the organisation is paying for the coaching they receive. This reminds clients that it is a professional arrangement. If a client wants to see me outside scheduled meetings, I remind them that they or their company will be charged for the time involved for additional face-to-face work.

The issue of the relationship remaining professional throughout extends to the fact that an executive coach will in all probability be privy to information of a sensitive nature. Perhaps it will entail knowledge that may affect the stock price of a company, or something equally important that must remain confidential.

If, for example, I own shares in a company that hires me, I always declare that fact well in advance and I will not buy or sell shares in that company until after an acceptable period following the end of the coaching relationship.

An executive coach has a responsibility to take no advantage, pecuniary or otherwise, from the relationship with a client other than the payment agreed. If conflicts of interest arise – for example, coaching two clients who are in competition with one another – this conflict must be declared and resolved, even if that means referring one client to another coaching organisation.

Client obligations

While much of the implied contractual responsibility lies with the coach, some responsibility falls on the client. It is useful at the start of a coaching relationship to make the client aware of this. Much of the client's responsibility relates to whether or not they will allow the process to be productive.

In order for that to happen, the client must 'buy into' the coaching. This means they should have some advance knowledge or perception of what the coaching process entails. They must be aware that for the programme to be effective they need to be honest about their thoughts, feelings and their vision. Also from the onset of the course, they must feel comfortable with their proposed coach and that coach's background.

There is absolutely no point in entering into a coaching programme with a client who does not want to be coached. Sustained resistance will frustrate both participants, and will provide little or no benefit to the client or the client's company.

Part of the 'buy-in' required from the client is recognition that they too must try to ensure that coaching will have a positive impact. That will certainly happen if they proactively participate and seek positive outcomes. How might they 'proactively participate'? The first requirement is openness of mind. They need to be aware that – notwithstanding the skills of their coach – much of the benefit they will derive from their time with their coach depends on the level of thought and commitment they invest in the process.

In order to sharpen their performance in the work place, a client needs to accept that there is room for improvement. They must be prepared to look at things from a different standpoint and they have to want to profit from the coaching. This may sound obvious, but it is sometimes surprising how many people enter into an executive coaching programme without making any commitment to the process, or without working for the results that will make it a success.

In my company, we always insist that potential clients meet at least two of our coaches so the client can choose the coach they are most at ease with. During these chemistry meetings, a discussion takes place about what the client and their organisation wish to achieve from the coaching. In the course of this meeting, or early on in the first coaching session, a dialogue will take place about how long the coaching relationship will last, how it will end and what a successful outcome from the programme might look like.

Other tools that could help the coaching process may also be discussed, such as the possibility of using 360-degree reviews, observation of the client in the work place, the provision of client appraisals and the possibility of the coach seeking feedback from colleagues prior to the start of the coaching. There should also be total clarity and transparency at this time in respect of the fees to be charged for the coaching programme.

Protecting a client's career

Most clients come to sessions with a lot to moan about. They have gripes about their bosses, their colleagues and the organisation for which they work. More often than not, they have a fundamental belief that the grass is greener on the other side of the fence.

This usually means they have persuaded themselves that they would get better recognition, more opportunity and greater reward if they moved to a different company. Occasionally, even the coach may conclude that they could be right. However, coaches are not there to encourage a client to move jobs. They are there to help clients perform better in their current jobs. Coaches also have a huge responsibility to protect their careers.

There are countless people who have resigned from good jobs where they were fundamentally happy because they thought they would enjoy a swifter climb up the career ladder in another firm. People who think that way have usually put some feelers out and only make the move if they hear encouraging noises from rival firms.

Unfortunately, some people have not even made elementary preliminary enquiries. They just assume they will find a suitable post once they are free. Or, worse, they have become so emotionally wound-up about their current position that leaving seems to be the only sensible solution. When employees get into that state of mind, logic deserts them. Usually they have not given any real thought as to what they will do next. These are all potentially fatal errors in a client's career.

If someone is not happy in their current job, the best way out of it is via promotion. That means that they need to be good at what they do, to meet and surpass expectations so they can move up. Only rarely is it the answer to simply leave one job and go in search of another. It is always easier to find a job when you are already in one!

Even a client who has been offered a job elsewhere should understand that they will go through a probation period during which they are risk of being 'let go' with few rights or benefits. They are, after all, starting in a new organisation where they have to build political capital and credibility from scratch.

They may think their potential employer is going to be better than their present boss, but they will not know that for sure until they are actually working in the organisation. The old saying, 'better the devil you know....', is a salutary reminder that there are many risks associated with venturing into unknown territory. It is often useful to remind clients of this.

Clients also need to recognise that if a potential employer is offering greater rewards, it will probably be in return for higher expectations. Perhaps it could mean more travel away from home, longer hours, or more stress. While the money may be attractive, do the duties and responsibilities involved fit with the client's values and aspirations? And, fundamentally, job seekers should never forget that a new post does not exist until a legally binding contract has been signed by the potential employee.

As a cautionary example, I can tell you of a client who thought she had secured a position with a new organisation. She resigned from her old job and agreed a departure date. But she had not signed a contract with the new employer. Between handing in her notice and the supposed start date of the new job, the potential employer had a change of mind. Suddenly, the girl found she was unemployed and had to start job hunting from a position of distinct disadvantage.

Business experience

It is stating the obvious to say that having extensive business and life experience are invaluable components of a good coach. The real value of any executive coach is founded in his or her business experience. Of course this is always something of a trade-off, as well as a subjective opinion. Coaches with a background in psychology would argue that years of training in that discipline are the key to the work, particularly as so many issues in business are relationship based.

Conversely, a coach with 20 or 30 years' experience in business, who has undergone a good academically accredited training programme, would insist that those skills are better suited to coaching within a business context. This is simply because few psychologists have extensive commercial experience. At the end of the day it depends on what the client wants and what works for them as an individual. There is merit in both arguments.

However, commercial experience is undeniably an extremely

important tool. A coach with wide experience of shareholder agreements, who is able to read accounts, knows the technical terms and implications of net present values, discounted cash flows or price-earnings ratios is speaking the client's language.

It is crucial to understand the fundamentals of business today – to know what shareholders expect, what issues relate to stakeholders, and what the law says about the responsibilities of executive and non-executive directors. It is equally important to be fully conversant with the direction in which business is moving. In today's world, the focus is on increased transparency and accountability.

I know it is important for a coach working with a bond trader or an investment banker to be familiar with most of the terminology of their professions, be it convertible bonds, yield curves, hedge fund phrases or the abbreviations related to mergers and acquisitions and valuations. This knowledge enables the client to talk about work without having to 'translate' what they are saying. In addition, the broader one's experience as a coach, the more options you might find for your client.

That certainly does not mean that the only person who can coach an investment banker is an investment banker turned coach. In fact, coaches with too much experience of one particular industry can easily be tempted to move into 'tell' mode, and that breaks the first rule of the profession.

As a coach, always remember why you are there – to help your client help himself. Never ever coach someone who doesn't want to be coached. At the end of the day, remember that most people's ultimate barrier to success lies in not having the bottle to go and see if it works.

Before you read on.....

As you can see from the above, there is more to being a good coach than honing the techniques that will allow you to coach well. You are also faced with considerable ethical and professional obligations. There will be times when you will be tempted to step over a boundary. This is particularly likely when coaching colleagues in politically charged work environments.

Please consider very carefully how you will shoulder and discharge these responsibilities. If you feel that you are the type of person who has trouble keeping information confidential, consider carefully how much coaching and what type of coaching you should undertake.

You may find it useful to make a list under two headings:

- As a coach I will:
- As a coach I will NOT:

You are now the guardian of a set of powerful psychological tools. Please respect the use of these skills.

11

Feedback – Looking At Results

*'You cannot teach a man anything. You can only help
him to discover it within himself.'*
Galileo

As a coach, and therefore someone who is likely to give others
feedback with relative frequency, it is important that you are yourself
open to feedback from those that you coach.

It is critical that you understand how you can gather the
appropriate information to feed back to your clients. Whether you are
coaching someone who works for you or an outsider, self-awareness
and sensitivity to feedback is essential.

Seeking feedback from your clients

In addition to asking clients to give me written summaries of our
sessions, I encourage them to comment on the coaching. This is
useful information for a number of reasons. Firstly, it is rewarding to
hear a client say they have truly benefited from a session. Often they
report new clarity of purpose or say they have attained a particular
goal that they would never have got without outside help.

Some say they now see their job differently, enjoy their work
more or that their improved performance has resulted in greater
appreciation and respect from colleagues or bosses. Others report
that coaching has encouraged a different way of thinking, which has
enhanced other aspects of their lives.

I also want to make sure that they are being frank and not simply telling me what they think I want to hear. I do this by observing them closely at this juncture, to pick up on any little tell-tale signs that suggest they are trying to please me. I need to be sure that I am making a real difference to their performance in the workplace, and therefore to their lives.

It is also useful to make them reflect on what they are getting from the course in order to reinforce the changes it brings about. It tells me how they now approach tasks, and the different methods they are adopting to deal with familiar issues. It is also likely that someone within their organisation is going to ask what benefit they have derived from our sessions. It is useful for a client to be prepared for the question.

Bearing testimony

As part of the executive coaching contract, a client agrees to provide a written testimonial that is 'content free'. This means that they comment on the overall effectiveness of the programme, without having to divulge any specifics.

Since we rarely see ourselves as others do, it can be revealing to get outside impressions and interpretations of our actions. It does not mean, necessarily, that we are wrong and they are right. But it is useful to have some subjective third-party opinions of who we are, what we think, say and do. Looking at our situation through someone else's eyes can tell us if we have been communicating well. Listening to outside opinion will soon show whether the messages we think we are getting across are actually being received in the way we intended.

Often we think that we are being clear and communicative when in fact the recipient's interpretation of the information is very different. Unless we seek to understand someone else's view of us we will always think that they have understood us, until – sometimes with shock – we learn that this is not the case. It can also happen that both parties remain blissfully unaware that a particular message has been totally lost – until our expectations are not met and we are left wondering what went wrong.

Difference of opinion

When five people summarise what they thought was said in a meeting at which they were all present, this can be an amusing exercise. In my experience, there has been more than one occasion when each of the five versions was so unlike the others that it seemed as if they had all attended totally different meetings.

The reason for this divergence is that we tend not to be good listeners. In order to add meaning and context to what someone else is saying we interpret their words through our own filters, beliefs and experiences. It is this process that can lead to misunderstandings.

Feedback can come out of a coaching session in many ways. The coach can observe a client communicating with colleagues, customers or bosses. For this to be effective, it is a good idea if he or she can sink unobtrusively into the background as an observer. It is usually necessary to ensure that the meeting or discussion in question is of sufficient length for the presence of the coach to be forgotten. It is also important for the coach to be satisfied that the client is talking unselfconsciously and spontaneously, rather than acting in a manner which suggests that he or she is aware of being observed.

After this meeting, the coach can give the client feedback and observations in private, offering them a very powerful and different overview, albeit only the reaction of one observer.

The full Monty

If a client wishes, the coach can take the experience further by carrying out a 360-degree review of the client, seeking feedback from people above, below and lateral to them. This can be done face-to-face, over the telephone or in the form of questionnaires. In this exercise, it is important for the coach, as always, to be clear about the objectives and the type of information being sought. It is also essential that confidentiality is respected for all concerned.

I also seek out as much reaction as possible from a client's company during the coaching process. For example, many firms now do annual reviews which the coach may be allowed to look over, in strict confidence. That is an effective way to identify areas where a client needs to change, in addition to revealing their strengths and capabilities.

Many highly successful people have a habit of haranguing themselves over imagined failures. They can be their own harshest critics and thereby greatly contribute to the erosion of their confidence and determination. It is sometimes healthy to acknowledge faults and weaknesses, but never to the point where they cannot tell when they have done something really well and should give themselves a metaphorical pat on the back.

Learning to be able to say 'well done' to oneself is fantastically productive in personal motivation. It is reinforced by feedback showing that from another person's perspective we have done well, even if we may not have not thought so ourselves. Feedback is frequently positive, as well as providing an indication of areas that need improvement.

Since much of executive coaching is about building confidence, it is extremely important to transmit the good feedback, as well as pointing out the opportunity for improvement which bosses or colleagues have suggested.

All external assessment leads to forward actions and change. It encourages people to use methods that work and to alter those that are ineffective. It helps a client to set goals and weigh up the consequences before acting. Above all else, it provides subject matter for reflection.

It is hard for most of us, given the frantic lives we all lead, to find the time and space to reflect about what we do, how we do it and where it is taking us. If we are able to create time and space to reflect on our performance, it is critical to have relevant information to work on. A coach will provide that to a client, but feedback from others allows for a more rounded set of subjects.

Long term effects

It is also revealing to compare responses from the same sources at the start and end of series of coaching sessions. This is a reliable measure of success. For example, the last exercise can be conducted a year after the programme has ended, in order to measure the sustainability of the lessons learned.

If the feedback is intended to measure the effectiveness of

executive coaching, it will be made up of both qualitative elements and quantitative measures, such as differences in profit and loss accounts. These are a reflection of all the factors that affect a business, not just the coaching quotient. However, it is usually possible to agree a factor of change to profit and loss that both client and company can identify as the result of coaching. That decision will obviously depend on a number of variables including historical volatility, market factors and peer result comparison.

A client is not the only one who will benefit from assessment. It is advisable for a coach to seek an evaluation of their own work and for a client to offer a personal opinion of the coaching they received to their colleagues, their organisation and the other people that surround them. This helps to ensure best practice since a coach's reputation hinges on feedback from their clients to potential clients. It is also important because if a coach's methods are not working, the sooner they are aware of that and change their approach, the sooner positive results will be created.

One of the great arts of leadership is to know when to listen. The Hay Group, the US-based professional services firm, points out that corporate leaders need resilience and emotional intelligence above all else. It also says leaders need to listen carefully at all levels. It is vital for a potential leader to develop the listening skills needed to hear feedback with an open mind. Then they can deliberate on it and create forward-looking action plans.

Don't procrastinate

There is no point in knowing the things about ourselves that need improvement unless we take action to improve them. When we make a commitment to someone else to take action there is a vastly improved chance that we will actually do it.

When my clients decide on a course of action I always ask them to specify the time this will take place or the date on which it will be completed. I do not impose the time frame. It is decided by them. I then wait until shortly after the date, and go back to check that it has been completed. It only takes a few missed, self-imposed deadlines before the client, knowing that they will be asked, sticks to the tasks and the timetable.

There are so many occasions in our lives when we know exactly what action to take, but we procrastinate. Exercising can be a classical example. We know we should do it, and we know that once we are sufficiently motivated to begin, we enjoy it. Even so, we fail to exercise as frequently or regularly as we know we should. On the other hand if we arrange to go for a hike with a friend or to meet someone at the gym, lo and behold we find ourselves there with remarkably little effort.

The same commitment and timeframe is necessary for executives to carry out tasks in the work place. On one occasion I found myself thinking I should write a letter to the *Economist* commenting on an article they had published about executive coaching. I had thought about doing so the previous day too. When one of our coaches then called me on another subject and I mentioned my plan, he asked when I was going to write the letter. I told him I would do it there and then and, having committed myself to the deed, I felt obliged to get on with it. I am not sure the letter would have been sent had that conversation not taken place.

Once I had written it and copied my colleague by email, he did what every good coach would do – he congratulated me. In our organisation, we actively seek clear actions and an appropriate time-table to make sure plans are carried through. So much of our supervisory and quality assurance work relies on observation and feedback. We practise what we know works.

I am one of those people who think things take longer than they do in reality. I have now started to measure the difference between my perceptions and reality. I began this the day I walked into my kitchen and found there was washing up to do. As can sometimes happen, the little task seemed harder to carry out than anything else. I decided to boil the kettle and reward myself with a cup of tea as soon as I had done it. I washed up, and there were fewer dishes than there had seemed. To my amazement, the kettle had not boiled by the time I had finished. I was struck by the way tasks can seem so much bigger to us than they really are. It started me thinking about what I was putting off that I could swiftly tackle by getting the right perspective on what was really involved.

It dawned on me then that I had far less reservation about writing this book than I had when I saw dirty dishes at the sink. Yet one was a tiny domestic duty, which would take a few minutes. The other was an undertaking for which I had no previous experience, and which would claim months of my spare time in a highly pressurised career.

Environmental feedback

That thought made me assess other aspects of daily life. I realised that marketing the executive coaching services of Thomas Preston and Associates seemed less daunting than getting my business cards printed. I saw that I wasn't putting things in their rightful context in terms of time and effort. Once I actually started to take note of that fact, everything began to get much easier. I call this 'environmental feedback'. It can be useful to put smaller actions into perspective.

Some people worry at the prospect of seeking out feedback. They fear the possibility of 'negative' responses, or unfair or biased criticism. I understand this point of view. However, I have come to believe that there is no such thing as negative feedback. If someone tells me I am doing something badly I usually already know that, even if it is on a subconscious level. More disconcertingly, I recognise that it is something I have previously chosen not to change.

Sometimes the feedback I get is a surprise, but only rarely. I usually know when I have done something really well and can tell when the reaction I am getting is genuine. This can be a very useful lesson and more often than not I am grateful for all and any feedback I receive. There is one proviso which I stipulate, and that is that the feedback is fair and genuine. It must not be designed to hurt, and cannot be fabricated. Feedback is valuable only when it is done for the right reasons.

The actions that result from feedback can have a remarkable effect. There have been a number of times when I have seen people persuaded of their ability to do something, simply because someone else has told them that they can do it.

I have also seen the reverse. Some time ago I suggested to a long-time contact that she should become an executive coach. I knew that the person concerned had all the right qualities and the business

171

experience that would be enhanced by proper training. I also thought that she would truly enjoy the process of coaching.

When I suggested this, my friend was amazed. She didn't think that she would get through the rigours of the training programme and felt sure she wouldn't know how to deal with clients.

As we talked, I assured her I thought her experience and personality were well suited to the profession. As she processed this information she started to see it as possible; something that she was capable of doing. A few days later, she came to see me again. She had done some research on the training programme and she thought it looked interesting. She investigated further and found that her credentials and experience did indeed qualify her. Bit by bit she decided that she wanted to train.

It happened that I was presenting on the programme that she attended. She was animated, diligent, absorbed and very much one of the stars of her group. It was remarkable to see someone getting so much out of something they had previously thought they could not do. And all because, initially at least, the feedback they received had made them believe that they could do it.

Hamstrung by history

The converse can also be true. If someone constantly hears others telling them that they cannot do something, that is likely to become a self-fulfilling prophesy. I have watched perfectly capable people becoming unable to do the simplest task because someone at some point has told them that they were not equal to it. What a shame it is that people can have their lives and careers handicapped merely because they are stuck in a sea of belief arising from outside opinions that may not be true, well-intentioned, relevant or helpful.

Relevant feedback will, usually, spur us to appropriate action that can help us to perform better, open our options and choices to provide us with better solutions and improve the quality of our lives and our performance at work.

Feedback is a tool not just for coaches but for everyone, from friends and colleagues to family.

Before you read on.....

Consider what feedback you would like to have as a coach. What information would help make you an even better coach? How would you want to be told about some of your more sensitive development areas? If, taking an extreme example, you had an infection in your mouth and as a consequence had very bad breath, but were unaware of this, how would you want to be told? It is vital that you have heightened self-awareness when giving or receiving feedback.

For a moment, reflect carefully on how you will handle these challenges.

12

Tangible Benefits

'It is never too late to be what you might have been.'
George Eliot

When I finished my own training as an executive coach I was convinced that the special techniques that I had learned were seriously under-utilised in the world of business.

However, having such a personal conviction without having empirical evidence to back it up can lead to a lack of confidence which undermines the arena within which a coach operates.

By now, you should be certain that executive coaching is indeed a magical management tool – a gift. Yet, even though you will have thought in depth about the various issues surrounding coaching, you too may still be sceptical about just how beneficial it can be to the wide world of business.

Well, consider the following: if you could bring about in your work place the kind of improvements in performance that we have discussed in these pages, would you have more confidence to be a champion of executive coaching?

Want proof of the results?

As a manager or shareholder of a business, how much would you be prepared to invest to achieve overall improvement in the performance of executive staff? Before you make a decision, consider the following:

Of staff who undergo executive coaching the percentage who report benefits are:

- Improved relationships with direct reports – 77%
- Improved relationships with managers/boss – 71%
- Improved relationships with peers – 63%
- Increased job satisfaction – 61%
- Increased organisational commitment (less likely to leave) – 44%
- Improved relationships with customers – 37%

(Source: Manchester Consulting – results of a survey of coaching at senior executive level in Fortune 500 companies)

Employees who benefit from the investment also report:

- Improved self awareness – 67.6 %
- Better goal setting – 62.4%
- Better work/life balance – 60.5%
- Lower stress levels – 57.1%

(Source: International Coaching Federation, IFC)

If all that improvement resulted in a more positive attitude within your organisation, plus greater productivity and performance, in turn yielding improved profits and stakeholder value, what would it be worth to you?

Obviously these improvements are highly valued by the managers and shareholders of any organisation. The key lies in the equation between the cost of the investment and the amount of return.

I am not aware of any major quantitative studies on the returns achieved from executive coaching but I have seen empirical evidence. I have to rely on the feedback from clients and the clients of other coaches. This evidence suggests that the economic benefits of executive coaching are far greater than the surveys suggest.

Return on investment

Obviously the bigger the turnover of an organisation the greater the potential return, irrespective of whether the organisation is profitable or not. Frequently a company that is losing money needs this type of investment in order to move it into profit. This is particularly true in organisations that need to go through restructuring or other substantial changes before there can be any improvement. It is also necessary in any company where morale is low and when new vigour is needed to produce positive results.

Talent, the underlying factor in producing profits for any company, is also something that must be developed and nurtured in order to derive maximum benefit from it. All organisations seek the top talent executives so it follows that they are harder to retain, as the best people are constantly being tempted by better offers from competitors.

Losing talented people in whom a particular company has invested years of training is extremely expensive due to the replacement cost. Any cost effective investment that significantly increases the chances of retaining such talent must be seriously considered and valued.

There are various studies assessing the cost of stress to national economies and in every one the figures over any single year are staggering. The higher up an organisation and the greater the level of responsibility a person shoulders, the greater the potential cost implication of stress. Again, if executive coaching can reduce stress, and I believe it does so remarkably effectively, why would a company be reluctant to make the investment in its senior people?

In my own firm we have developed tools to measure the return on investment from coaching, in order to prove to clients that they get back many times the cost of their investment. For example, one client recently concluded that the return on investment was 32.5 times the cost of the coaching programme.

One of the great advantages of executive coaching is that it can be used in almost any organisation, irrespective of the sector. It is flexible and, unlike management consulting, the solutions to issues come from the people that know the organisation best – those that run it.

Let's look at a couple of case studies.

Media business

I worked with an Asian-based media business that achieved cost savings of US$400,000 per year and moved from a significant loss to a profit of 10% of turnover through group coaching of the board of directors. However, the figures alone do not show the full value of coaching that was the initial factor in moving the company from loss to profit.

In addition, the creation of profits allows companies to invest in critical parts of their business, making them stronger and more competitive and thereby adding shareholder value in the short and long term. Profits allow companies to pay the competitive rates of remuneration, which helps them to retain and attract key staff, as well as improving the quality of life for those who work for them. This in turn makes for higher morale and better performance.

So the coaching of the media company, that brought about a US$400,000 cost reduction and return to profit, actually resulted in a far greater return on investment than the figures suggest.

Clothing manufacturer

There is a telling case history from one fashion organisation with which I worked. The company elected to spend money on coaching their board of directors in order to address two key issues. They wanted to establish the road map for an eventual sale of the business for £20 million.

The critical questions they had were: How could they achieve this? And what were the individual roles and responsibilities that ensured each director was contributing in the best way possible to reach the ultimate goal?

Through the coaching process, a five-year business plan was established with clearly defined quarterly and yearly goals for profits and turnover. This allowed the directors to measure at any given point where they were on their road map to sale. It also acted as a guide for the decisions and actions that needed to be taken in order to ensure they reached their goals. It forced them to define the core offering of their business and to analyse the profitability of each function of the company. This enabled them to redefine their sales focus to ensure they were generating the highest possible margins. It further allowed the board to develop tools to continually measure the shape and form of their business in line with the profitability of the separate functions.

'Now,' I hear you say, 'that's not executive coaching, it's the simple basics of good business practice.' And yes, that is true. However, as many venture capitalists know, entrepreneurs tend not to have the self-imposed discipline to do a *realistic* five-year business plan. Many managers of small and medium-sized businesses find it hard to conduct a personal reality check. Their drive to realise their dreams often prevents them from carrying out the cold, hard objective analysis that needs to be done by any business in order to prosper. Neglecting to do this is often the cause of failure in these businesses.

An executive coach acts as the catalyst for this analysis to ensure that entrepreneurs focus on and carry out the necessary planning, management information system implementation and strategic thinking that is so vital to progress. Unfortunately, it is something they might otherwise not do as a consequence of being consumed by the day to day demands of running a business.

With this particular company, we identified ways they could improve their current year profits by £200,000 to £700,000 while increasing their turnover by only £500,000. In other words, they improved their profit margins through the coaching process.

After agreeing a five-year business plan it became clear exactly what responsibility each director needed to assume, and what role and job function they needed to perform in order to arrive at their five-year goal. Essentially, this resulted in greater performance and productivity from the company's most expensive assets – its directors.

So, in the case of this relatively small company, its £20,000 investment in executive coaching produced short-term profits of £200,000 and made it far more likely for the board to achieve its long-term goal of selling the business for £20 million. Quite how one calculates the total return on such an investment I am not sure, but on the surface it looks pretty good to me.

Venture capital and private equity

The example above is also one reason why executive coaching is such a useful tool to the venture capital and private equity communities. I used to run a private equity firm and the issue I constantly faced was getting entrepreneurs to understand the needs and objectives of financial investors, and *vice versa*. Entrepreneurs are emotionally attached to their businesses and, while they want an investor's money, they frequently resent the imposition of discipline that comes with it. Often they argue that financial investors fail to understand their business. This can lead to serious discord, but, if explained and discussed in a different way, the outcome could be productive and beneficial to both sides.

Take the example of the child who will accept advice proffered by a favourite uncle yet reject it when given by his father. In this case the child is the entrepreneur, the father the financial investor and the executive coach the favourite uncle.

Large multinationals

I worked with a client who provided an interesting example of the power of coaching and the potential economics for business on a large scale. This client is an extremely talented young, but senior, executive who is the number two running a global division of a FTSE 100 company. As his coach, there was little I could do to improve his technical performance. He was already at the top of his game.

However, he devised an initiative to produce better returns on capital invested in the business. The plan showed that more targeted and directed use of capital could free up substantial sums of money while maintaining the same returns the company was achieving from the capital currently employed.

However, in order to implement the initiative, my client needed the support of a broad spectrum of stakeholders, ranging from the main board to the teams in different countries that would be charged with the implementation of his proposal.

In order to help him manage this process, we created a stakeholder map. The map listed the various people and teams that would be involved in the initiative. It detailed what my client needed to do to get their attention and support. It also listed the potential obstacles and resistance that might arise and suggested how best to handle the situation if it arose. The plan worked on various different approaches designed to avoid sparking the negative sensitivities that such an innovative plan could provoke within the stakeholder group, the industry or the financial markets.

Once that was done, the client said he was far more confident that his initiative would be adopted and it has since been implemented successfully,

In what way can the input of a coach in this example be quantifiably valued? The client was the genius behind the initiative. When questioned, he knew what he needed to do and precisely how to do it. As his coach, I simply acted as a prompt, asking some probing questions. And yet, my client's company has reaped the benefit from the release of over £100 million of capital for use in the rest of its business, with no downturn in profits or cash flows. That might not have happened had they not hired a coach to help the executive work through the entire process. Ultimately, this initiative resulted in significantly improved return on investment for the shareholders.

Team results

Teams, as has been proved over centuries in sport, derive huge benefit from coaching. Teams that are cohesive, supportive, goal-oriented and focused simply produce better results. However, it is a huge challenge for any leader to create and maintain a cohesive, supportive, goal-oriented and focused team that operates at all times at peak performance. Coaching is a powerful tool to create these qualities in teams and thus get better results from them. In addition, compared to individual coaching, the cost is spread over several people, making it more economic on a per capita basis.

Recruitment

The best results I have seen come from a combination of team coaching and individual coaching of the team leader. Consider the results of a coaching initiative for the senior management team at Manpower Canada – Canada's largest staffing company.

The company conducted a coaching programme for six months, at the end of which the results were reviewed and analysed. The coaching was evaluated using a proprietary quality assurance process and a 360-degree feedback instrument, which linked to the desired leadership competencies at Manpower Canada.

The following response data indicate the level of satisfaction and represents a summary of the quality assurance feedback. The participants were interviewed at mid and end points of the six-month programme to determine the level of satisfaction with their progress in the eight identified areas as follows:

Response key

1. Have not realised any change.
2. I have realised some change.
3. My approach is noticeably different, as noted by me or others.
4. My approach has dramatically changed
5. N/A, not applicable

Summary of Results

	Percentage reporting an Improvement
1. Communication Average Score: 3.2	100%
2. Teamwork Average Score: 3.5	100%
3. Leadership Average Score: 3.2	100%
4. Innovation Average Score: 3.1	95%
5. Customer Service Average Score: 3.1	100%

6. Productivity   83%
   Average Score: 2.4

7. Goal Setting   100%
   Average Score: 2.9

8. Effectiveness   96%
   Average Score: 3.0

Professional practices

Professional practices, such as law firms and accounting practices have many of the same needs as other businesses. Frequently, professional practices are partnerships. Partners tend to stay with a firm over long periods of time, often until retirement and, like families, partnerships sometimes fall into bad habits formed over many years. Although this happens subtly and by such slow degrees that no-one really notices, it eventually prohibits their growth, stunts change and consequently inhibits their ability to produce maximum returns for their partners and stakeholders.

Coaching is extremely successful in helping partnerships regain direction, focus, change outmoded methods of working and rekindle energy. For example, many law firms suffer from the inability to cross-refer clients between disciplines and offices within their own structures. As a consequence, potentially huge revenues are lost.

Raising awareness of the skills and client bases that each partner has, focusing each of them on how they can personally market the partnership's range of disciplines to mutual benefit, and bringing back the origins of trust and pride that created the system of partnership in the first place, can significantly enhance the revenue that a partnership can generate from its existing client base.

This is generally a far better use of resources than the time, effort and expense of getting brand new clients from other marketing approaches, especially those that attempt to lever clients away from competent competitors with whom the clients have existing relationships.

I acknowledge that the executive coaching industry is still at a formative stage and there is insufficient data on the economics involved to substantiate the empirical evidence that I, and many others, have seen. However, the evidence strongly indicates that it improves business performance significantly.

Perhaps the most striking evidence is the fact that it has grown so rapidly from almost nowhere ten years ago in the United States. Is it possible that an industry could grow to this extent if it did not produce tangible results and offer good value for money? The same explosion is now happening across Europe where coaching is said to be the fastest growing industry after IT. Furthermore, it seems indisputable that this incredibly powerful performance tool is growing in credibility and here to stay. Despite the lack of scientific proof, logic suggests that the economic benefits are substantial.

Before you read on.....

I trust that you now feel more confident of the impact that you, as an executive coach, can make.

Before you turn to the last chapter of our journey together – thank you. Thank you for thinking deeply about all that you have read and learned.

Thank you for letting me, as your coach, stimulate your thoughts and actions.

It has been my pleasure to work with you but, like all good coaching relationships, ours must draw to a natural close. It remains for me simply to ask you a few more questions – but, by now, that will probably not surprise you....

13

The Gift

*'Suddenly I saw things differently, and because I saw
differently, I thought differently, I felt differently and I
behaved differently.'*
Stephen Covey

Now you have reached the final chapter of *Coach Yourself to
Success*. As I said in the introduction, this book is a gift to you. I
hope that you will come back to it time and again down the years,
reminding yourself of how you can access the very best of the
potential within you.

Every word has been chosen with infinite care to ensure that you
fully understand the gift of coaching – for yourself and for others.

With practice you will become a gifted coach. You will now
know how to make a real difference to your own life and to your own
performance. And, most importantly, you will know how to make a
real difference to the life and performance of those around you. You
have a remarkable gift not only to enjoy, but also to share.

Yet now you have to make a fundamental life choice. We know
that the road to success and happiness starts with choosing to be so.
But are you ready to make that choice? Are you sure that you want
success and happiness *enough* to think differently, to do things
differently, to listen differently, to question more thoroughly and to
search for the very best options?

Are you willing to audit your beliefs and to change those that are
not useful to you? Are you prepared to accept that the one certainty

in life is change and that therein lies opportunity? Can you visualise yourself at the peak of your potential – achieving more than you ever thought possible?

Will you invest in teams in a different way, will you change course when something is not working? Will you listen with your eyes, your intuition and with silence, as well as with your ears?

Will you recognise that viewing other people with unconditional positive regard shakes off the yoke of being judgemental and offers you the ability to pass on the gift to others? Will you act in a way that develops the talent in others?

Will you hold the mirror up to others in a way that is designed to positively impact that person's life – providing the person with the feedback that gives them the opportunity to learn and become a richer person?

Will you respect the boundaries and confidences of others when you share your gift with them? Will you share it at every possible opportunity?

But first ask yourself this question: do you want to have more fun and greater rewards from life *enough* to do these things?

If you do want these, how will you get them?

And what will you do, and when, to ensure that you get what you want?

Before you make these fundamental choices, can I suggest that you now write a letter? It is ten years from today's date. Write to someone you totally trust. Imagine that you are looking back to the present and that in the interim you have lived a perfect life (within the bounds of reality – remember, no magic!).

Begin by describing where you are while writing the letter. Then, as if you are counting backwards to the present, describe the events that led you to where you are. As you look back over the past ten years to the present, outline the major milestones you see. And remember – it has been your perfect life.

Then make that choice.

Index